DATE DUE

NOV 1 2005		
DEC 2 7 2005		
APR 1 5 2006		
NOV 2 7 2010		

amco, Inc. 38-293

"There is really no such thing as bad weather, only different kinds of good weather."

– John Ruskin

Weather!

By Rebecca Rupp

With journal illustrations by Melissa Sweet
and experiment illustrations by dug Nap

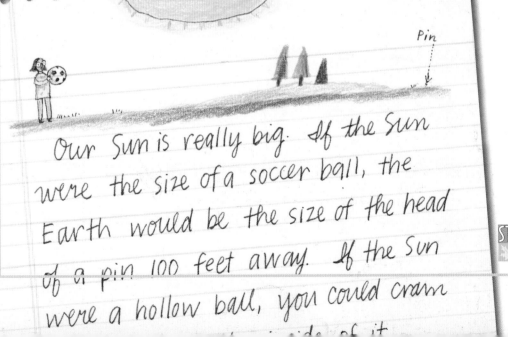

Our Sun is really big. If the Sun
were the size of a soccer ball, the
Earth would be the size of the head
of a pin 100 feet away. If the Sun
were a hollow ball, you could cram

STOREY
KIDS

The mission of Storey Publishing is to serve our customers by publishing practical information that encourages personal independence in harmony with the environment.

Edited by Deborah Burns

Designed by Wendy Palitz

Text production by Stephen Hughes and Kelley Nesbit

Cover photographs © Bettmann/CORBIS (front); Frog image © Photodisc/Getty Images

Interior photography credits listed on page 135

Infographics © Judy Sitz: 11, 21, 25, 27, 29, 46, 69, 85, 100, 109, 118-119 adapted from Dorothy A. Wallace-Senft's collage of W. A. Bentley photographs; and by Stephen Hughes: 7,17, 47, 80, 87, 108, 110, 131.

Indexed by Susan Olason/Indexes & Knowledge Maps

Special thanks to John Hockridge, New England Weather Associates

Jemima and Rodney's journal illustrations © Melissa Sweet

Projects and experiment illustrations © dug Nap

Printed in China by Regent Publishing Services

10 9 8 7 6 5 4 3 2 1

Library of Congress Cataloging-in-Publication Data

Rupp, Rebecca.
    Weather! : Watch how weather works. Featuring 22 experiments for making your own rain, tornados, lightning, and rainbows, with plans for cool weather gizmos! / Rebecca Rupp.
        v.   cm.
    Includes bibliographical references and index.
    Contents: The atmosphere: What's up? — Wind: huffs, puffs & hurricanes — Sunshine: beams, burns & blue skies — Clouds: white sheep & little cat feet — Rain: drops, drizzles & downpours — Thunder & lightning: Thor's hammer & Zeus's spear — Snow & ice: frost, flurries & blizzards — Predicting the weather: reading the skies.
    ISBN 1-58017-469-8 (hardcover) ISBN 1-58017-420-5 (alk. paper)
    1. Weather—Miscellanea—Juvenile literature. [1. Weather—Miscellanea.] I. Title.
QC981.3 .R87 2003
551.6—dc21
                          2002152310

Contents

I have decided to keep a weather journal.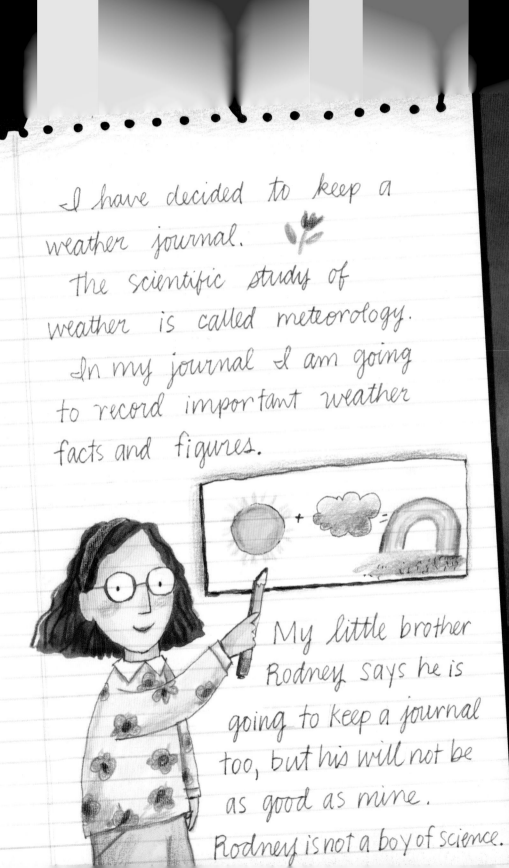

The scientific study of weather is called meteorology.

In my journal I am going to record important weather facts and figures.

My little brother Rodney says he is going to keep a journal too, but his will not be as good as mine.

Rodney is not a boy of science.

I have decided to keep a weather journal too. It will be like Jemima's except mine will be better.

Jemima has no imagination.

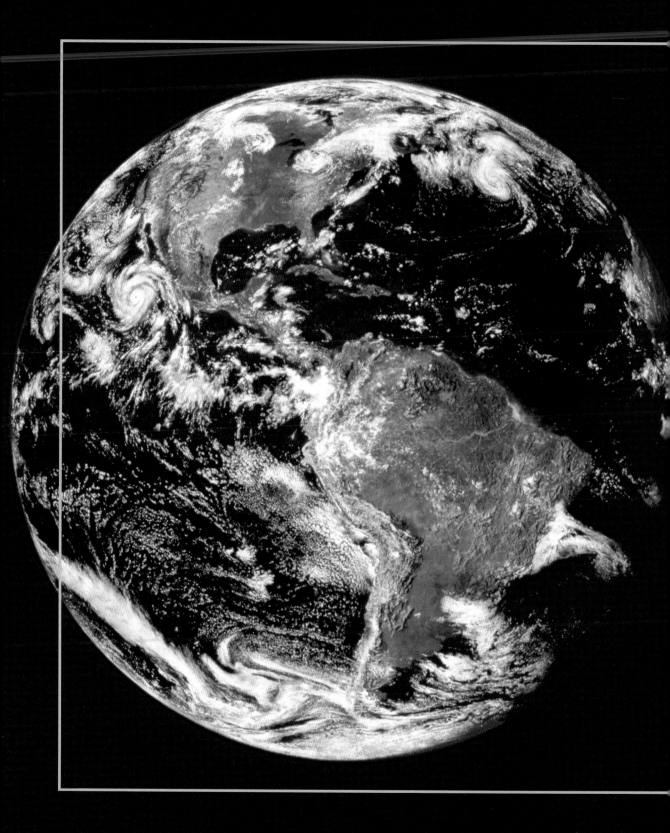

Chapter One

"All sorts of things and weather
Must be taken in together,
To make up a year
And a sphere."

– Ralph Waldo Emerson

The Atmosphere

What's Up?

We all live at the bottom of an enormous global swimming pool filled with 5,000 trillion tons of air. Every moment of every day each one of us staggers under a 300-mile-high column of air that shoves down on us with a force of 14.7 pounds per square inch. Lie down flat and you're being squashed by 15,000 pounds or so of air — about the weight of one full-grown elephant or three hefty cows. The amazing part of this is that we barely notice it.

Not-So-Empty Air

We're designed to live in Earth's air, nicely adjusted to the peculiarities of our planet. Remove the atmosphere, on the other hand, and we'd all be in terrible trouble. Deprived of oxygen, bombarded by ultraviolet radiation, and abruptly depressurized, our bodies would swell up, our eardrums would explode, our blood would boil, and we wouldn't last seconds.

An **atmosphere** (literally, "sphere of air") is defined by scientists as the envelope of gases that surrounds a planet. Not all planets have one. Some are too small and therefore have too little gravity to hold an atmosphere in place. Some are too hot, so that all the surface gases have boiled away and vanished into outer space. Mercury, for example, is both: With gravity only about a third that of Earth and a scalding location 57 million miles closer to the sun, Mercury has no atmosphere at all.

Neither does the Moon, which is smaller yet. Mars, just half the size of Earth, has a thin unbreathable atmosphere consisting mostly of carbon dioxide. Venus's atmosphere, which is 96 percent carbon dioxide topped off with sulfuric acid, helps make it the hottest place in the solar system. Surface temperatures on Venus hover around 900°F, hot enough to melt lead. Jupiter and Saturn, both massive spheres of hydrogen and helium gas, are practically *all* atmosphere, and Uranus and Neptune are wrapped in hydrogen, helium, and methane. Pluto has a barely detectable atmosphere of nitrogen and carbon monoxide.

Earth's atmosphere, in contrast, is crammed full of stuff. Air contains 78 percent nitrogen, 21 percent oxygen, and 1 percent argon and other gases, such as krypton, hydrogen, carbon dioxide, neon, methane, helium, and xenon. Most of this is concentrated in the portion of the atmosphere closest to the Earth, the layer you're sitting, standing, or running around in at this very moment. Meteorologists call it the **troposphere**.

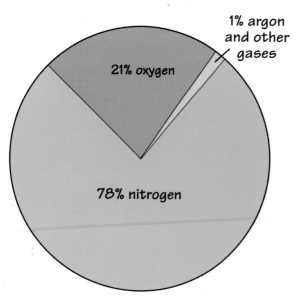

1% argon and other gases

21% oxygen

78% nitrogen

Air is mostly nitrogen and oxygen, but it also contains tiny amounts of argon and other gases.

Take a Deep Breath

Each of us breathes about ten million times per year, taking in about five million liters of air — enough to fill three hot-air balloons.

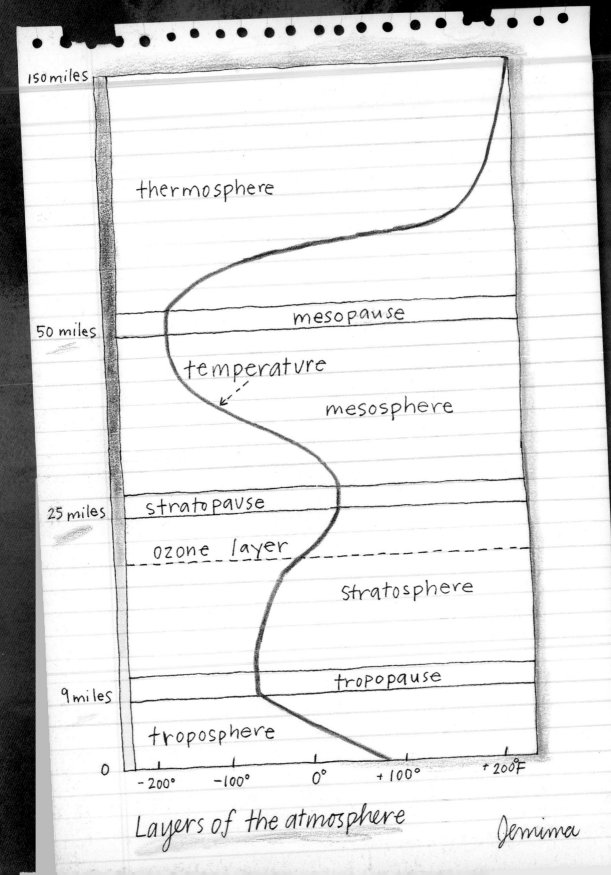

Layers of the atmosphere

Jemima

northern lights

aliens

space
shuttle

thermosphere
------- 50 miles
mesosphere

meteors
burn up

Santa's
sleigh

Stratosphere ------- 25 miles

weather
balloons

jet
plane →

hot air
balloons

Troposphere - - - 7 miles

earth

our
↓ house

Mt. Everest

highest bird
flight

Rodney

Slices of Sky

When it comes to weather, the **troposphere** is where it's at. It contains weather's raw materials: the lion's share of the Earth's oxygen and other gases, the bulk of the water vapor, most of the clouds, and practically all of the world's wind. The troposphere is about six to seven miles high over the temperate zones, ten miles high over the equator, and five miles high at the poles. At the very top of the troposphere is the **tropopause,** a layer that acts much like an invisible ceiling in the sky.

The tropopause is cold. In the troposphere, temperature drops with altitude, steadily getting colder the higher you go. By the time you've climbed to the top of Mount Everest (29,035 feet above sea

Sunglasses Overhead

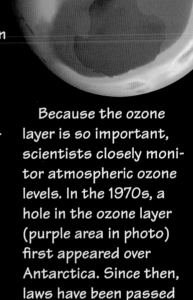

Most of the oxygen atoms in our atmosphere exist as twins. The stuff we breathe is O_2, diatomic oxygen, a two-atom molecule. Ozone (O_3), however, is a triplet. That extra oxygen atom makes a big difference. Oxygen is colorless, odorless, stable, and safe; ozone is blue, has a peculiar piercing odor (the name comes from the Greek ozein, meaning smell), and is barely stable. In fact, when condensed into liquid form, ozone explodes.

Ozone in the stratosphere benefits us just because it's unstable. Highly reactive molecules of ozone absorb ultraviolet (UV) radiation from the Sun before it can reach and damage living things on Earth. UV radiation is dangerous because it zaps biological molecules like DNA, killing cells or causing cancers. The ozone layer acts like a pair of protective sunglasses in the sky, shielding us all from destructive glare.

Because the ozone layer is so important, scientists closely monitor atmospheric ozone levels. In the 1970s, a hole in the ozone layer (purple area in photo) first appeared over Antarctica. Since then, laws have been passed banning the use of ozone-damaging chemicals, but the problem is far from solved.

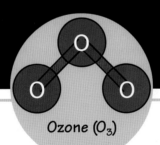

Ozone (O_3)

level) the temperature will have dropped by about 104 degrees. At the tropopause, temperatures can plunge to a tooth-chattering –60°F.

If you head higher, though, and enter the **stratosphere,** your surroundings become a little warmer. Here, 6 to 30 miles above sea level, the frigid subzero temperatures gradually increase with altitude, eventually reaching a relatively cozy 32°F, the freezing point of water. The air in the stratosphere is thin: There's so little oxygen, in fact, that it would be impossible to light a candle. Jet planes routinely fly through the stratosphere and it is home to the **ozone layer,** which protects the Earth from the sun's ultraviolet radiation.

Heavenly Heights

At the top of the stratosphere is the **stratopause,** which is unexpectedly warm (32°F) due to the heat generated by the energetic ozone layer. The next layer of the atmosphere is the **mesosphere,** which extends from about 30 miles to 50 miles above the Earth's surface. Temperatures are cold up here:

Meteor

they can dip to a mind-numbing –160°F at the upper limit of the mesosphere, the **mesopause.** Meteors generally burn up in the mesosphere. These are the blazing rocks that observers on Earth sometimes call falling stars.

Above the mesopause is the **thermosphere,** extending from 50 to 400 miles above the Earth. Its name comes from the Greek word for heat, which makes sense because the thermosphere is by far the hottest of the Earth's atmospheric layers. Though there's not much air — the thermosphere contains only a tiny fraction (1/100,000) of the atmosphere's gas molecules — those few molecules absorb enough of the Sun's radiation to boost temperatures to more than 3,000°F.

The upper reaches of the thermosphere are called the **ionosphere** because this atmospheric layer is filled with electrically charged particles called **ions** — molecules whose electrons have been stripped away by solar radiation. These ions, interacting with the Earth's magnetic field, create glorious auroras, visible over the poles as the northern and southern lights.

The final and outermost layer of the atmosphere is the **exosphere.** This begins 400 miles or so above the Earth's surface and extends outward some 40,000 miles, gradually merging into the depths of space. The exosphere is empty. Down in the crowded atmosphere, gas molecules can barely move three-millionths of an inch before crashing into a neighbor; in the exosphere, lonely molecules of hydrogen, helium, and oxygen can drift forlornly for as much as six miles without meeting another soul.

Feeling Pressured?

The force of all these atmospheric layers pressing down on everything beneath them is called **atmospheric pressure.** Atmospheric pressure depends on altitude: that is, the higher up you go, the less pressure there is, because there's less air to push down on top of you. Your ears pop when you're in a car driving up a mountain because of pressure differences. As you go higher, the air pressure pushing in on your eardrums from the outside drops until it's less than the pressure pushing out from the inside. The imbalance makes your ears feel funny.

Air pressure also changes continually on the surface of the Earth. When air heats up, its trillions of gas molecules start leaping around faster and faster, which makes the blob of heated air swell and expand. This hot air weighs less than the cooler air around it, so it exerts less pressure on the surface below. **Low-pressure zones** are created by masses of warm air bobbing up over the ground like huge lightweight balloons. **High-pressure zones** result from heavier, colder air hunkering down on the Earth's surface like oozy sacks of mud.

Air pressure differences mean moving air. Air always moves from regions of high pressure to regions of low — and the greater the pressure difference, the faster it moves.

We have a special name for moving air. We call it "wind."

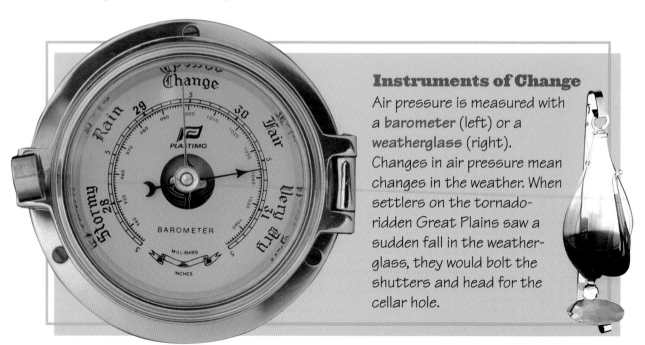

Instruments of Change

Air pressure is measured with a **barometer** (left) or a **weatherglass** (right). Changes in air pressure mean changes in the weather. When settlers on the tornado-ridden Great Plains saw a sudden fall in the weatherglass, they would bolt the shutters and head for the cellar hole.

Measuring Air Pressure

Air pressure, the force with which the weight of the air presses down on the Earth, can be measured either directly (as in how many pounds of air there are for every square inch of surface area) or indirectly (as in how many inches a given amount of air pressure boosts the mercury in a barometer). All measures of air pressure — direct, indirect, English, and metric — are related to one another.

The higher up you go, the less air there is pushing down on you, so the air pressure is less.

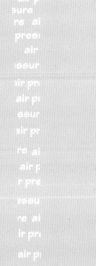

Torricelli's Tricky Tube

The barometer was invented in 1643 by an Italian mathematician named Evangelista Torricelli, a onetime student of Galileo. His new device, originally known as "Torricelli's tube," was basically just that: a long glass tube filled with mercury, sealed at the top and open at the bottom. As air presses on the reservoir at the open end of the tube, mercury is forced up the tube until it reaches a level where its weight precisely balances the weight of the pushing air.

MAKE YOUR OWN BAROMETER

What you'll need:

- A small coffee or salted-nut can
- Plastic wrap
- A large rubber band
- A drinking straw
- Tape
- A blank index card

1. Cover the top of the can with a sheet of plastic wrap. Fasten tightly in place with the rubber band. The plastic wrap should be stretched taut and the can should be airtight.

2. Lay the straw horizontally across the top of the plastic wrap so that about one third of the straw extends over the end of the can. Tape the straw to the middle of the plastic wrap.

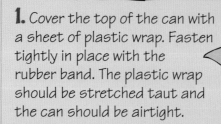

3. Tape the blank index card to the side of the can so that it extends out behind the straw.

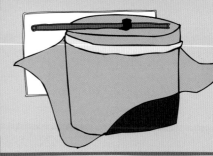

4. Draw a line on the index card to mark the starting position of the straw.

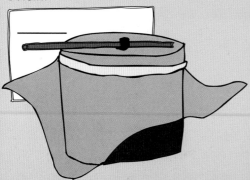

5. Continue to check the position of the straw at intervals.

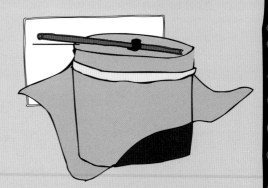

What happens: High air pressure will push down the plastic wrap and will cause the straw to move up. Low air pressure will cause the plastic to puff up and the straw will move down.

The Big Squash

What you'll need:

- An empty aluminum soda can
- A hot plate or stove
- Tongs
- A shallow pan or dish containing about an inch of cold water

Get a grown-up to help you with this one!

1. Pour a spoonful of water into the soda can.

2. Place the can on the hot plate or stove and heat it until steam begins to escape from the opening on top of the can.

3. Lift the hot can with the tongs and place it upside down (open-end down) into the dish of cold water.

4. Watch the SQUASH.

What happens: When the can is upended in the cold water, the hot air inside the can cools. As the air cools, the water vapor will condense, forming water droplets on the inside of the can. As the water vapor condenses — leaving the air — the air pressure decreases inside the can. When the air pressure outside the can becomes greater than the pressure inside the can, the can is crushed.

Chapter Two

"Day-long, night-long, the cool and pleasant breeze
Of the steady Trade Winds blowing."

— John Masefield "Trade Winds"

Wind

Huffs, Puffs & Hurricanes

According to the ancient Greeks, the winged god Aeolus kept all the world's winds in underground caverns on a floating island in the Mediterranean Sea. In *The Odyssey* by Homer, Aeolus gave Odysseus a leather bag full of winds to take on board his ship on his way home from the Trojan War. Odysseus always kept the bag tied shut, but one day, when he fell asleep, his men opened it and let all the winds out. The ship was caught in a terrible storm, and everybody except Odysseus drowned.

A Boiling Pot of Air

In time, curious people began to devise natural (though sometimes rather peculiar) explanations for the happenings in the world around them. The Greek philosopher Aristotle proposed that the wind was the dry breath of the Earth. He believed wind was trapped underground and, when heated by friction, sometimes exploded out of volcanoes. The Roman naturalist Pliny the Elder guessed that the wind fell from the stars.

Modern scientists now know that wind is moving molecules of air, and the movement of those molecules ultimately depends on the Sun. The Sun warms the Earth unfairly. Earth is hottest around the middle at the equator, where the most direct rays of the Sun fall, cold at the neglected poles, and warmish in between. These differences in temperature cause air to move.

Hot air is lighter than cold air, which means that warmer air floats upward, bobbing toward the upper reaches of the atmosphere like a huge, shapeless, toasty balloon. As the hot air over the equator rises, it leaves a hole beneath it, a gap that meteorologists refer to as a **low-pressure zone.** Cool, heavy, low-lurking air from neighboring higher or lower latitudes promptly rushes in to fill the hole.

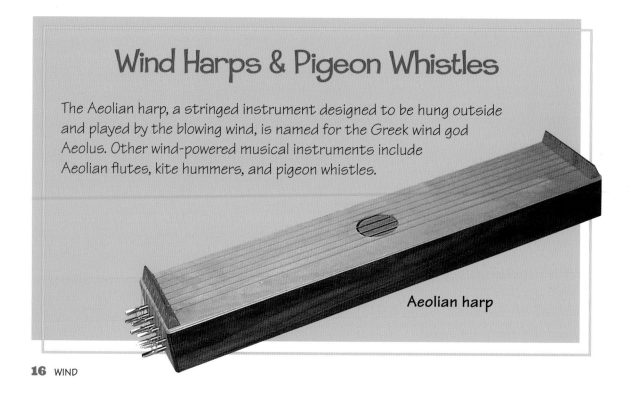

Wind Harps & Pigeon Whistles

The Aeolian harp, a stringed instrument designed to be hung outside and played by the blowing wind, is named for the Greek wind god Aeolus. Other wind-powered musical instruments include Aeolian flutes, kite hummers, and pigeon whistles.

Aeolian harp

This cool air, itself warmed by the blazing equatorial Sun, soon begins to rise in its turn, pushing the air above it either north or southward. As the pushed air is shoved into the cooler upper (or lower) latitudes, it cools off and starts to sink, forming a high-pressure layer of heavy cool air, poised to rush in again and fill the gap left by warm air rising upward over the equator. The huge wheeling circular path that the air follows in the course of this warming and rising and cooling and falling is called a **convection cell.**

Convection happens when anything fluid — air, water, chicken noodle soup — transports heat from someplace hot to someplace cold. Convection is why water boils in a pan on top of the stove. The water closest to the stove burner gets hot, which causes it to become lighter (less dense) and to rise toward the top of the pan. There it meets the outside air, cools down, becomes heavier, and sinks back to the bottom of the pan to be heated, and the whole process begins again. It's this temperature-driven circulation that eventually brings water to a boil.

FACT! Kite fighting is a popular sport in eastern Asia. The goal is to entangle your opponent's kite and force it down. Fighting kites of bamboo and paper or silk can need 20 adults to maneuver.

Convection

Convection doesn't occur in the absence of gravity. If you tried to boil a pot of soup in gravity-less outer space, the water at the very bottom of the pot would eventually reach the boiling point, but the water on top would stay cool.

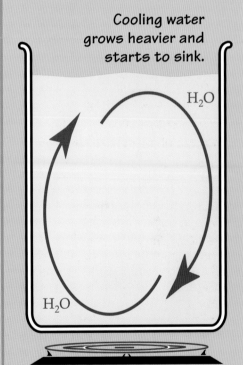

Cooling water grows heavier and starts to sink.

H_2O

H_2O

Heated water grows lighter and starts to rise.

As water (or air) heats up, it begins to rise. As it cools, it grows heavier and sinks, filling the gap left by the rising warm water.

Rodney has been running around all day with a pillowcase talking about catching the winds in a bag.

He is nuts.

I have explained to him that nobody can catch wind in a bag because wind is simply air moving from areas of high pressure to areas of low pressure.

But Rodney does not seem to believe me.

Jemima

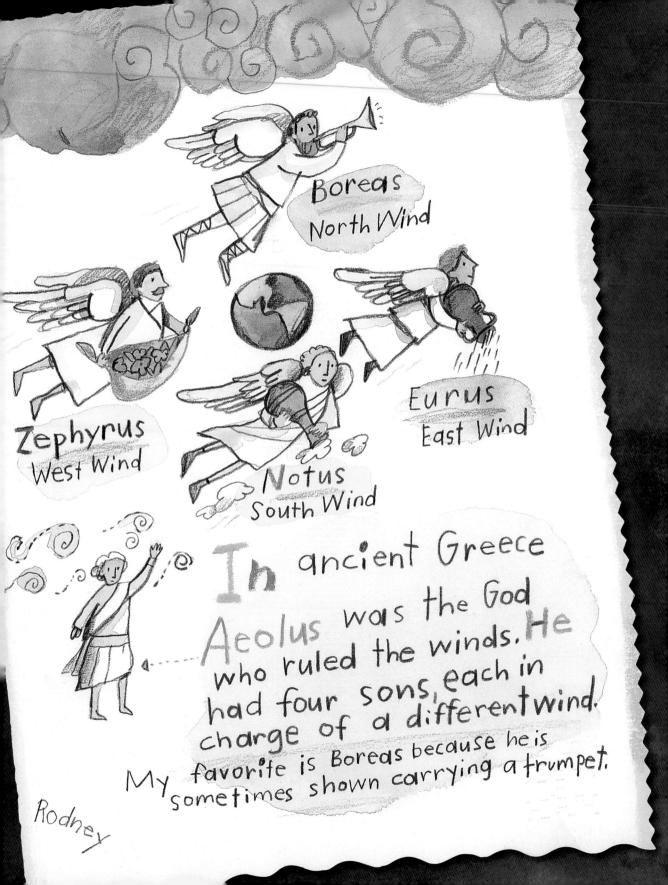

Boreas
North Wind

Eurus
East Wind

Zephyrus
West Wind

Notus
South Wind

In ancient Greece Aeolus was the God who ruled the winds. He had four sons, each in charge of a different wind. My favorite is Boreas because he is sometimes shown carrying a trumpet.

Rodney

Merry-Go-Round in Space

The Coriolis effect is easiest to understand if you imagine trying to walk off a moving merry-go-round. If you walk straight across the floor of the merry-go-round, heading (you hope) for the exit gate, you find that the motion keeps carrying you forward, beyond where you want to go. Similarly, the winds, in their paths across the spinning global merry-go-round, end up being pulled sideways.

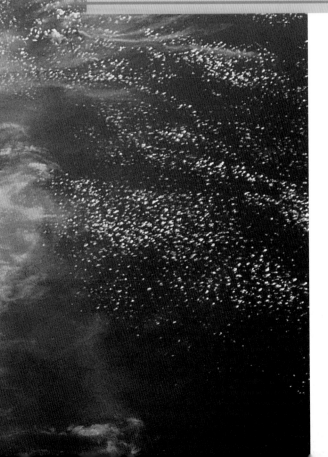

Spin Cycle

The Coriolis effect is all the fault of the Earth's rotation. The west-to-east spin (1,040 miles per hour at the equator) nudges traveling objects (including wind) off course, deflecting them to their right in the northern hemisphere and to their left in the southern hemisphere.

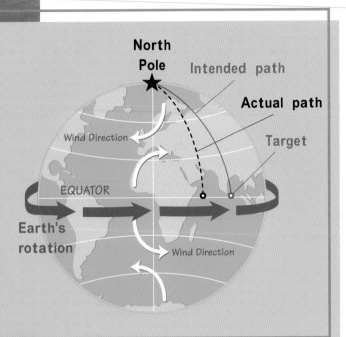

North Pole

Intended path

Actual path

Target

Wind Direction

EQUATOR

Earth's rotation

Wind Direction

The wind doesn't just move up and down and north and south. It also moves sideways. It's forced to, because the Earth never stands still. Instead, our planet spins like an outsized top, twirling around on its axis once every 24 hours, rocketing west to east at more than 1,000 miles per hour, about as fast as a jet plane flies.

Air, heading north from the equator, for example, gets pulled right (to the east) as the Earth rotates rapidly along beneath it. This dizzy process of being yanked off course as you try to move in a straight line across a rotating object is called the **Coriolis effect** after Gaspard Coriolis, the French scientist who discovered it in the early 19th century.

The Compass Rose

The ancient Greeks recognized four different winds: Boreas, the north wind (an angry-looking brute with a trumpet); Zephyrus, the west wind (carrying an armful of flowers); Notus, the south wind (pouring rain out of a jar); and Eurus, the east wind (gloomy). Later, eight more winds were added, bringing the total up to twelve.

At first there was a lot of confusion over just what to call all these rapidly multiplying winds, but mapmakers eventually settled on a system based on the cardinal points of the compass. The primary winds were thus named north (N), south (S), east (E), and west (W), while the winds that fell awkwardly in between the cardinal points were given combination names. A wind that was positioned midway between north and east, for example, became a northeast (NE) wind, or if it was northeast but closer to the north, it became a north–northeast (NNE) wind.

Winds are always named for where they're coming from. A west wind blows out of the west and heads east, and a north wind roars out of the north and heads south. The arrow on the weather vane always points directly into the wind — that is, toward its direction of origin (the direction in which you shouldn't spit).

Feathers, Roosters, Banners, and Socks

Devices for determining the direction of the wind have been around for thousands of years. The Polynesians used feather pennants tied to the rigging of their canoes; Viking ships carried flat bronze weather vanes, shaped like quarter-circles, held on poles.

In medieval Europe, long cloth banners were flown from castle towers to show archers the direction of the wind. (Our word vane, as in weather vane, comes from the Anglo-Saxon fane, meaning banner or flag.) These banners were later replaced with sturdier metal vanes, often topped with a metal rooster, or weathercock. Weathercocks first appeared in the 9th century A.D., after Pope Nicholas I decreed that all churches in Europe should display a cock on the roof in memory of Jesus' prophecy that the cock would not crow in the morning until his disciple Peter denied him three times.

Later weather vane makers came up with all kinds of variations on the

By the Middle Ages maps were illustrated with elaborate "wind roses," picturing up to 32 different winds.

traditional rooster. Paul Revere had a codfish weather vane on his silversmith's shop in Boston. Thomas Jefferson, at windy Monticello, connected his weather vane to a pointer on the hall floor so he could tell which way the wind was blowing without stepping outside of the house.

Today, windsocks (funnel-shaped tubes of fabric tethered to a pole) are often used as wind direction indicators.

Windy Planet

The looping paths of the world's winds form six major convection cells, three in the northern hemisphere, and three in the south. The cells closest to the equator are called the **Hadley cells;** those in the middle latitudes are known as the **Ferrel cells;** and those in the far north and south, bordering the North and South Poles, are called the **polar cells.**

The Trade Winds

When hot air rises over the equator, cool air from the middle latitudes rushes in to fill the gap and then is dragged sideways by the Coriolis force. These Hadley cells create, in the southern hemisphere, a steady southeast wind, and in the northern hemisphere, a northeast wind. These were known as **trade winds** since they transported merchant ships to the rich New World in the 1600s.

The Equatorial Doldrums

This no-man's-land of almost windless territory between the northern and southern Hadley cells was known to meteorologists as an **intertropical convergence zone** and to early sailors as the **doldrums.**

The Westerlies

North (and south) of the Hadley cells are the Ferrel cells. Sailors bound for India and the Spice Islands once rode the prevailing west winds of the Ferrel cells to maneuver around Africa's Cape of Good Hope.

The Horse Latitudes

This band of relatively still air was once known as the **horse latitudes** because it was here that, helplessly becalmed, sailors were forced to throw horses and other livestock overboard to save on limited supplies of drinking water.

The Polar Easterlies

North (and south) of the Ferrel westerlies blow the coldest winds of all, the **polar easterlies,** heavy with frigid air drifting south from the Arctic (or north from the Antarctic).

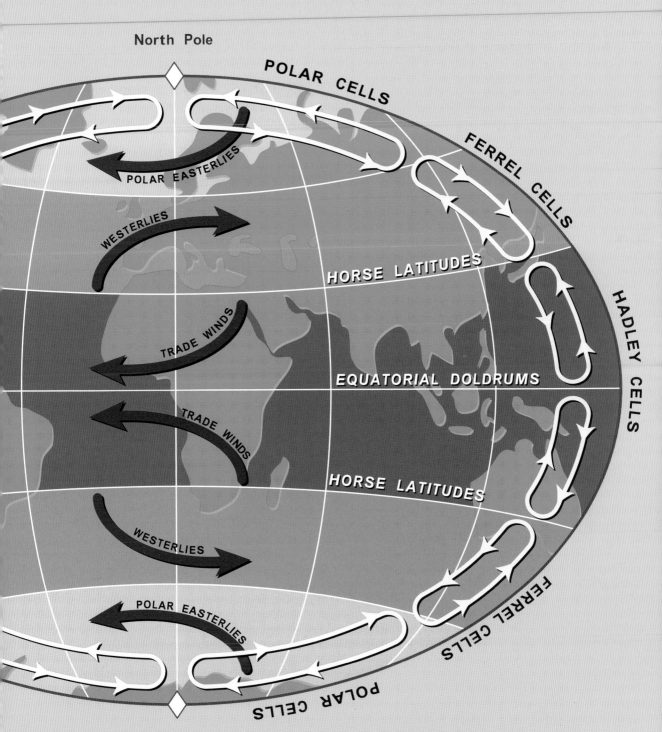

North Pole

POLAR CELLS

FERREL CELLS

POLAR EASTERLIES

WESTERLIES

HADLEY CELLS

HORSE LATITUDES

TRADE WINDS

EQUATORIAL DOLDRUMS

TRADE WINDS

HORSE LATITUDES

WESTERLIES

FERREL CELLS

POLAR EASTERLIES

POLAR CELLS

South Pole

Air, There & Everywhere

Most of the world's winds hug the ground. Almost all wind is found in the atmosphere's bottommost layer, the troposphere, five to ten miles thick depending where you happen to be on the surface of the Earth. The exceptions are the **jet streams** of the stratosphere, four great speeding rivers of air that zip around the globe 25,000 to 40,000 feet above the ground, following the junctions between hot and cold masses of air.

The jet streams were discovered by pilots during World War II, many of whom were horrified at encountering winds powerful enough to make their planes stand still at an altitude where no wind was expected at all. Jet stream

Going Up?

Wind changes with terrain, rising or falling, changing direction, braking or picking up speed depending on what it's blowing over. In part, this has to do with how well the underlying surface stays warm. Playgrounds, parking lots, and deserts, for example, become hotter and stay hot longer than fields and forests. Hot air, rising up in columns over extra-toasty portions of ground below, forms **thermals,** supportive updrafts of wind often ridden by soaring birds such as hawks.

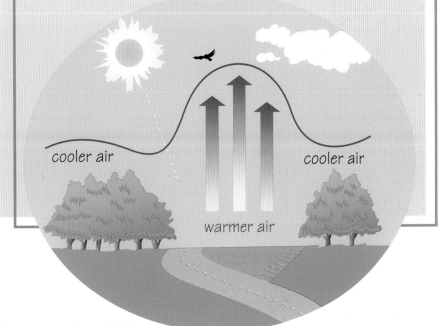

cooler air   cooler air

warmer air

winds range from 50 to more than 200 miles per hour. Today commercial airliners ride these "superhighways of the sky" to save time and fuel.

Land heats and cools more quickly than water does, which is why the wind at the seashore flip-flops daily. During the day, heated air rises over the rapidly warming land and the cooler air from over the sea swoops in to take its place. The result is a steady sea breeze, blowing inland all day long. In the evening, the process reverses: The land cools quickly and its now colder and heavier air moves offshore, edging under the warmer lighter air over the water creating a land breeze blowing out to sea.

Somersaults in the Sky

The wind is shaped by the ground. Wind washes over the Earth's surface the way water runs over a rocky river bottom. Just as an uneven riverbed will create ripples, waves, and wild white water on the river surface, the lumpy shape of the land creates waves in wind. When flowing wind hits an obstacle, the result will be **turbulence,** a somersaulting mishmash of air currents up to three times higher than the obstruction.

Obstacles slow wind down. Mountains are massive speed bumps for the winds. In the American Midwest, winters are fierce because North America has no sheltering west to east-running mountain range to block the freezing wind from the North Pole.

The wildest winds on the Earth blow across the middle latitudes of the landless south Pacific, thousands of miles of wind-whipped water between 40 and 60 degrees of latitude that whalers once referred to as the roaring 40s, the howling 50s, and the screeching 60s. It's these roaring, howling, and screeching winds that made it so difficult for sailing ships to round South America's Cape Horn.

Tied for windiest place on land are Mount Washington in New Hampshire and East Adelie Land, Antarctica, both of which average year-round winds of 40 miles per hour, with gusts raging up to 200 miles per hour or more.

You can estimate wind speed by using the Beaufort Wind Scale (right).

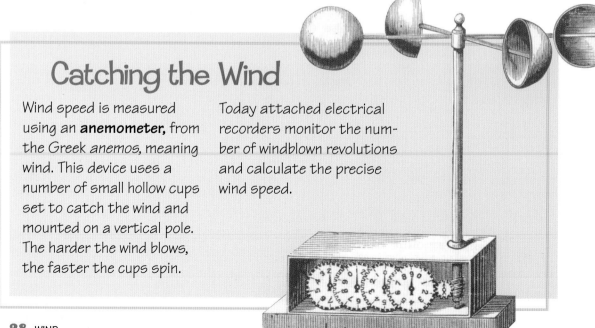

Catching the Wind

Wind speed is measured using an **anemometer,** from the Greek anemos, meaning wind. This device uses a number of small hollow cups set to catch the wind and mounted on a vertical pole. The harder the wind blows, the faster the cups spin.

Today attached electrical recorders monitor the number of windblown revolutions and calculate the precise wind speed.

Beaufort Wind Scale

Beaufort Number		Average MPH	Wind Effects
0	Calm	0	Smoke rises vertically
1	Light air	1–3	Smoke moves slightly with breeze; small ripples on water
2	Light breeze	4–7	Leaves rustle; weather vanes move
3	Gentle breeze	8–12	Leaves and twigs dance; flags ripple
4	Moderate breeze	13–18	Dust and paper blow; small branches move; flags flap
5	Fresh breeze	19–24	Small trees sway; crested wavelets on lakes
6	Strong breeze	25–31	Large branches sway; powerlines whistle; hard to use umbrellas
7	Moderate gale	32–38	Large trees sway; hard to walk against wind
8	Fresh gale	39–46	Twigs break from trees
9	Strong gale	47–54	Branches break from trees
10	Whole gale	55–63	Trees uprooted
11	Storm	64–73	Widespread damage
12	Hurricane	74+	Widespread devastation

Wind speed today: 4 miles per hour.
Rodney and I flew our kites. I
explained to Rodney that you do not
have to run to launch a kite. If one
person holds the kite angled into the
air while the other person lets out the
kite string, the wind will take the
kite up. But Rodney did not
believe me. I think Rodney
just likes to run.

ALL ABOUT AIRFOILS

Kites fly because they are **airfoils:** that is, objects, shaped to split the air unevenly while moving through it. Other examples of airfoils are bird wings, airplane wings, sailboat sails, and boomerangs. The air moves more rapidly over the top of the airfoil than the bottom, creating a pressure difference that results in an upward boost called **lift**.

Jemima

Today Jemima and I flew our kites. I helped by running, Jemima just stood there. Sometimes I think Jemima does not know how to have fun

Here are some of my favorite kites:

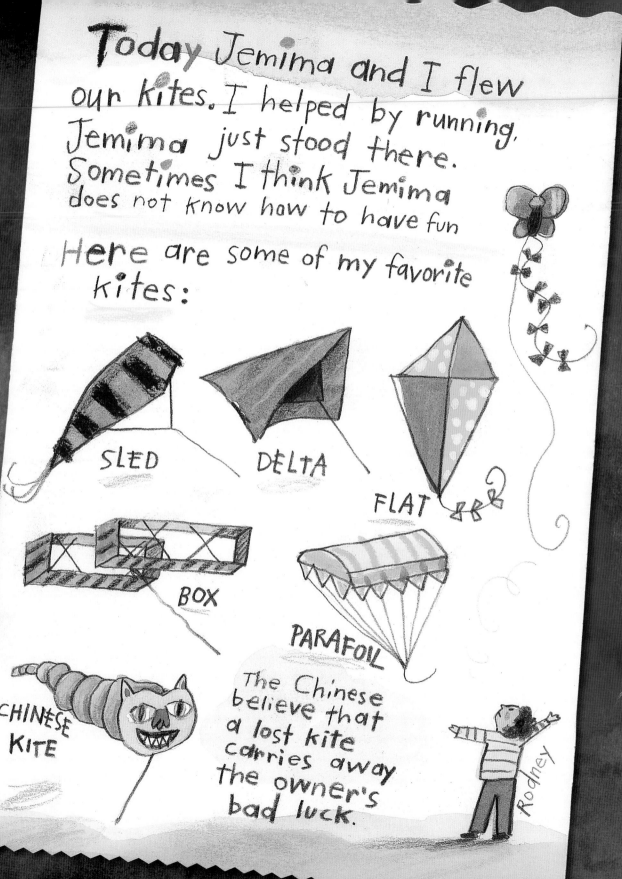

SLED

DELTA

FLAT

BOX

PARAFOIL

CHINESE KITE

The Chinese believe that a lost kite carries away the owner's bad luck.

Rodney

Wrath of the Weather God

The most horrific winds — number 12 on the Beaufort Scale — are hurricanes, named for the Mayan weather god Huracan, who devastated the Caribbean with storms whenever he was angry. Huracan's tantrums are awesome, storms capable of unloading a thundering 20 billion tons of water a day and traveling thousands of miles, all accompanied by roaring winds of up to 250 mph. A hurricane is 1,000 times more powerful than a tornado, the weather equivalent of 1,000 simultaneously exploding 20-megaton atom bombs.

Hurricanes are rated on the Saffir-Simpson Damage Scale, in which storms run the gamut from Category 1 (minimal) through moderate (2), extensive (3), and extreme (4) to Category 5 (catastrophic). By this assessment, even a minimal hurricane is bad news, and the more powerful storms are horrendous.

After Andrew

Hurricane Andrew (shown here), which devastated southeast Florida in 1992, causing $26 billion worth of damage and costing 23 lives, was a Category 4 hurricane. The cyclone that struck the coast of Bangladesh in 1970, killing 300,000 people, was a Category 5.

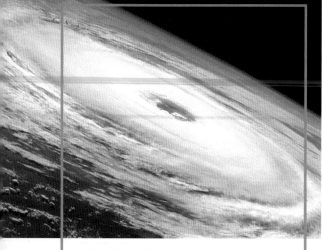

The Caribbean hurricane season officially begins each year on June 1 and ends on November 30.

infant hurricane grows, the incoming air begins to spiral upward, spinning faster and faster, egged on by the rotation of the Earth. (In the southern hemisphere, hurricanes spin clockwise; in the northern hemisphere, counter-clockwise.) When the swirling winds reach a speed of 39 mph, meteorologists — getting nervous — declare the disturbance a **tropical storm** and give it a name. When the winds reach 74 mph, the storm becomes a full-fledged hurricane, and any people unlucky enough to be in its path are warned not to be.

Hurricanes that develop in the Indian Ocean are called **cyclones,** from the Greek for "circle"; those that begin west of the International Date Line are known as **typhoons,** from the Chinese for "great wind." By whatever name they're called, they're killers.

Hurricanes don't look like much to begin with. They start innocently enough as low-pressure spots in hot tropical oceans. As the hot, humid air rises, a low-pressure zone develops beneath it and begins hungrily sucking in air. As the

A Hurricane Called Harvey

Hurricanes often occur at the same time and always move around. This was once confusing for weather stations, because they could never be sure who was talking about which storm. The problem was solved first by numbering hurricanes and later by giving them names.

Before 1979, these were always female names, but since then the National Hurricane Center has alternated between male and female names in alphabetical order. The names are recycled every six years, and some are occasionally replaced as the names of particularly awful hurricanes are retired.

If your name is Barry, Cindy, Dennis, Harvey, or Isabel, you're on the Atlantic hurricane list, along with Kyle, Mindy, Ophelia, Pablo, Richard, Sam, and Walter.

Naming hurricanes after people
helps meteorologists because
the names are easy to remember
Rodney is not a hurricane name.

Neither
is Jemima.

Putting Wind to Work

Scary as hurricanes are, the winds aren't all bad. Without wind, about 90 percent of Earth's plants would not be able to reproduce. These **anemophilous** or wind-loving plants depend upon the wind to distribute their pollen each growing season. The wind scatters the globe each spring with 100 million grains of pollen per square mile. Many plants also depend upon the wind to distribute their seeds — among them the tumbling tumbleweed, the fluffy-headed dandelion, orchids (all 15,000 species), milkweeds, sycamores, Scotch pines, and maples, whose double-winged seeds are designed to twirl through the air like tiny helicopters.

Human beings have utilized moving air to drive everything from clipper ships to windmills. Wind helped the Polynesians colonize the Pacific and powered the great Age of

Milkweed seed

Exploration of the 15th and 16th centuries, blowing Vasco da Gama to India, Columbus to the Americas, and Magellan all the way around the world.

Since ancient times, people have used wind power to pump water or turn grindstones. The ancient Persians used wind power to grind grain. The famous windmills of Holland were used to prevent flooding, pumping water out of the fields and into canals.

Wind Words

If you happen upon a **windfall,** you've just lucked into money; if you **get wind of something,** you've found something out. If somebody **takes the wind out of your sails,** your self-confidence has just been squashed; if you're **long-winded,** you talk too much.

On the other hand, if you know **which way the wind blows** — which you should by now — that means you're pretty clever.

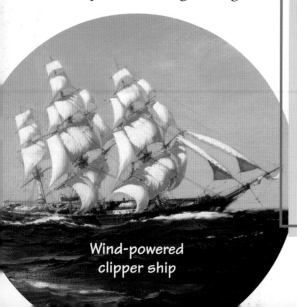

Wind-powered clipper ship

Farming the Wind

There's a lot of energy in wind. Scientists calculate that wind turbine farms located in the windiest parts of the United States — places where annual wind speeds average about 16 miles per hour — could supply more than 20 percent of our country's electricity.

Atmosphere in a Pan

What you'll need:

- A flat glass cake or bread pan
- Water
- A stove
- Food coloring

Get a grown-up to help you with this one!

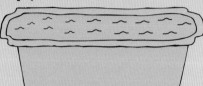

1. Fill the glass pan with water.

2. Place one end of the pan over the stove burner. Turn on the burner to low heat.

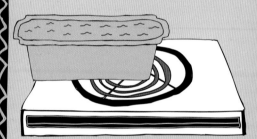

3. Add a few drops of food coloring to the cool end of the pan — that is, the end not over the burner. Do NOT shake or stir.

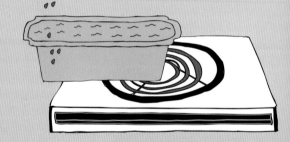

4. Watch the pan from the side.

What happens: You should be able to see a developing convection current as the colored dye sinks, moves toward the warm end of the pan, rises upward, and then moves back toward the cool end of the pan.

MAKE YOUR OWN COMPASS

What you'll need:

- A sheet of plain white paper
- A glass of water
- A small circle of paper or a slice of cork
- A sewing needle (careful; it's sharp)
- A magnet

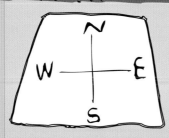

1. On the sheet of paper, draw a pair of crossed perpendicular lines. Label the ends of the lines N, E, S, and W (for north, east, south, and west).

2. Fill the glass with water and place it in the center of your diagram.

Make sure the letters are showing.

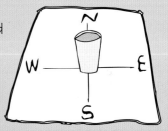

3. Float a small circle of paper or a thin slice of cork on the water in the glass.

4. Hold the needle by the eye – the non-pointy end – and stroke the magnet along its entire length, from the point toward the eye.

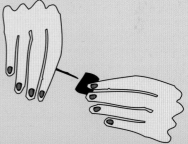

5. Place the needle flat in the center of the floating paper or cork slice. (Careful – don't sink it.)

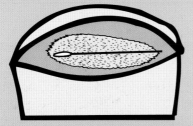

What happens: The magnetized needle should turn until its sharp end is pointing toward the north. Turn the labeled piece of paper under the glass until the N is in line with the needle. You now know the way to the North Pole.

Make your own Weathervane

What you'll need:

- A small wooden stick about 12 inches long and 1 inch wide
- An aluminum pie plate or lasagna pan
- A metal washer
- A dowel rod, ½ to 1 inch in diameter
- A large nail
- A small saw
- A drill
- Scissors
- Glue
- A hammer

GET A GROWN-UP TO HELP YOU WITH THIS ONE!

1. Cut a half-inch-deep vertical slit at either end of the 12-inch stick with the saw.

2. Drill a hole through the midpoint of the stick. (Measure to find the exact middle.) The hole should be larger in diameter than the nail.

Weird Winds

A **chinook** wind — named after a Northwest Indian tribe — is a sudden dry warm wind that rolls out of the mountains in winter, boosting the temperature by 50 degrees or more in minutes and melting the snow at the rate of an inch an hour.

The similar **foehn** wind of the European Alps is said to be hot enough to bake apples on the trees.

The **sirocco** is a hot dusty wind that blows out of Africa's Sahara Desert, and the **mistral** is a cold north wind that periodically shivers the coast of the Mediterranean Sea. New England has **nor'easters;** the Great Plains, **blue northers;** California has **Diablos** and **Santa Anas;** and Alaska has **williwaws.**

3. Cut a wide arrowhead and flat tail from the aluminum plate or pan. Glue the pieces securely in the vertical slits at either end of the stick.

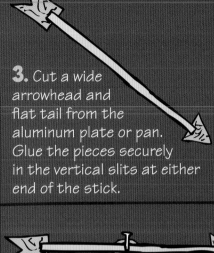

4. Place the metal washer on one end of the dowel rod. Fasten your weather vane to the dowel rod by hammering a nail through the midpoint hole of the vane and through the washer into the dowel.

Make sure your vane can turn easily on the nail.

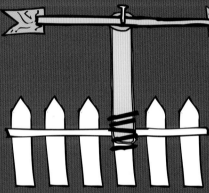

5. Mount your weather vane outside in an open area. For example, you might fasten it to a fence or porch railing with heavy tape or wire.

What happens:
When the wind blows, the arrowhead will point in the direction from which the wind is blowing.

MAKE YOUR OWN WHIRLACOPTER

1. Cut out strip of paper 4 inches by 1 inch and cut along solid lines as shown.

2. Fold along the dotted lines.

3. Hold stem upright and drop it from a high place.

"The Sun, with all the planets revolving around it and depending on it, can still ripen a bunch of grapes as though it had nothing else in the universe to do."

– Galileo Galilei

Chapter Three

Sunshine

Beams, Burns & Blue Skies

Our Sun is a pretty mediocre star. Everything about it is average. It's not too big or too small, too bright or too dim, too hot or too cold. And it's made almost entirely of just two elements, hydrogen (91.2 percent) and helium (8.7 percent), which for a star is nothing special. If our Sun were ice cream, it would be plain vanilla.

On the other hand, if it weren't for the Sun, none of us would be here. All life on Earth, from aardvarks and artichokes to zebras and zucchinis, owes its existence to the Sun.

Scatter!

When you look up into a clear blue sky, you're seeing short wavelengths of sunlight in action. When light enters our atmosphere after its eight-minute journey through space, it suddenly hits an obstacle — the thick soup of nitrogen, oxygen, and other gases that make up Earth's air. Light waves hit these gas molecules and bounce off, scattering wildly around the sky as if playing a gargantuan game of atomic pinball. Not all wavelengths, though, are scattered equally. Short wavelengths are scattered better.

Ordinary sunlight looks white, but it's actually every color of the rainbow, a mix of red, orange, yellow, green, blue, indigo, and violet. Red and orange light have the longest wavelengths; blue, indigo, and violet have the shortest. Because of its size, blue light is scattered much more efficiently than red light — and since there's so much more blue light scattering around, our sky looks blue.

This super-efficient scattering of short-wave light is called **Rayleigh scattering,** after the English physicist who discovered it.

Sunrises and sunsets look red, on the other hand, because they're composed of light leftovers. At sunrise and sunset, the Sun is so low on the horizon that light enters the atmosphere at a shallow angle in a long slanted path through the air. In fact, the light passes through so much air that all the short-wavelength blue light is scattered away altogether, leaving nothing visible but red.

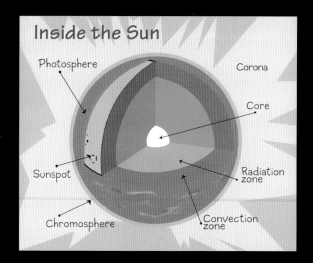

Inside the Sun

Photosphere · Corona · Core · Sunspot · Radiation zone · Chromosphere · Convection zone

The Orange Sky of Venus, the Pink Sky of Mars

Not all skies are blue. The sky from the Moon looks black because the Moon has no atmosphere. Without air, the incoming sunlight is not scattered at all.

The atmosphere on Venus, on the other hand, is so much thicker than Earth's that almost all the blue light is scattered away before it gets anywhere near the ground. The result is a red sky, tinged with yellow from sulfur in the clouds. The mix looks orange.

The sky on Mars is pink, from the reddish dust particles hurled into the atmosphere by Martian storms.

If you want to see blue skies, your best bet is Yuma, Arizona, which is the sunniest place in the United States, averaging 242 sunny days each year. Least sunny is Cold Bay, Alaska, with just ten annual sunny days, and all the rest of us fall somewhere in between.

With all that sunshine, Yuma can get hot. Its maximum recorded temperature is 124°F, just ten degrees cooler than the hottest temperature ever recorded in the United States: 134°F in Death Valley, California, on July 10, 1913. Hot, however, is relative. The hottest temperature ever recorded on St. Paul Island, Alaska, is a coolish 66°F; and summer on the coast of Antarctica reaches at best 59°F, which for most of us is sweater weather.

Since land heats and cools faster than water, landlocked cities suffer greater temperature extremes than coastal cities do. Landlocked Kansas City alternately bakes and freezes, while oceanside San Francisco has coolly pleasant weather year-round, though both cities are at the same latitude.

San Franciscans are in shorts while Kansans are in long johns because sunlight penetrates water so much better than it penetrates earth. Sunlight sinks only a few feet into the ground, heating just the very upper surface. (Underground caves stay cool.) On the other hand, sunlight can sink hundreds of feet into water. Water heats and cools more slowly because solar energy spreads out over so much of it. (Think of how long it takes a hot kettle of soup to cool compared to a hot flat cookie.) The slow heating and cooling of the ocean insulates coastal towns and cities against rapid changes in temperature.

Fahrenheit, Centigrade & Kelvin

Temperature is measured using three different kinds of scales. Most commonly used in the United States is the **Fahrenheit** scale, which divides the span of temperatures between the freezing point and the boiling point of water into 180 segments (**degrees,** symbolized by °). The freezing point of water is fixed at 32°F, and the boiling point of water is 212°F.

The metric system uses the **Celsius** or **centigrade** scale, dividing the stretch between the freezing and boiling points of water into 100 degrees. On this scale, water freezes at 0°C and boils at 100°C.

In the much larger **Kelvin** scale, zero is set at the coldest temperature possible: **absolute zero,** the temperature at which all molecular motion stops. 0°K is equal to −273.15°C or −459.67°F.

Here is my temperature graph.

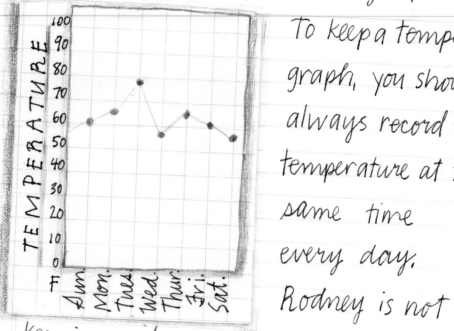

To keep a temperature graph, you should always record the temperature at the same time every day.

Rodney is not keeping a temperature graph. He does not understand temperatures.

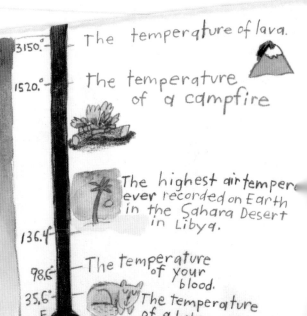

Jemima's temperature graph does not show very interesting temperatures.

3150.° — The temperature of lava.

1520.° — The temperature of a campfire

The highest air temperature ever recorded on Earth in the Sahara Desert in Libya.

136.4° —

98.6° — The temperature of your blood.

35.6° — The temperature of a hibernating squirrel's blood.

F

Hot Enough for You?

Temperature is measured with a thermometer. The most common thermometer used for monitoring weather is a bulb thermometer, which works because liquids shrink or swell depending on how cold or hot they are. Bulb thermometers generally consist of a narrow glass tube ending in a fat bulb, once usually filled with mercury but now more likely to contain alcohol. As the temperature becomes hotter, the liquid in the bulb expands, creeping out of the bulb and up the length of the tube. As it gets colder, the liquid contracts, takes up less space, and creeps back down the tube.

How hot the air gets depends on how much sunshine we actually receive. This varies, depending on the tilt of the Earth's axis, the position of the Earth relative to the Sun, and where we happen to be on the planet. Light from the Sun arrives at the Earth in neatly parallel rays and strikes the equator head on. However, because the Earth is a ball, sunlight hits the upper and lower latitudes at an angle. The sharper that angle, the less solar energy a given chunk of surface area gets.

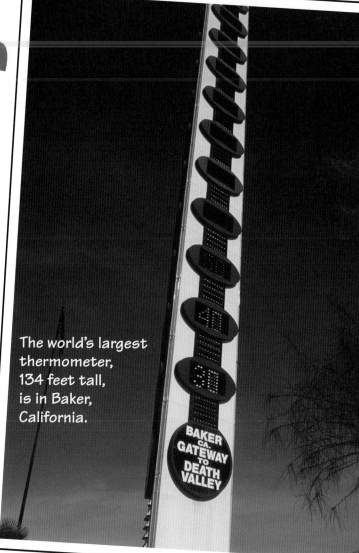

The world's largest thermometer, 134 feet tall, is in Baker, California.

FACT! San Diego, California, averages 146 sunny days per year; Tulsa, Oklahoma, has 127; Tallahassee, Florida, 102; Boston, Massachusetts, 98; Chicago, Illinois, 84; and Caribou, Maine, 59.

Then at certain times of year the Earth nudges closer to the Sun. Earth's orbit around the Sun is shaped like an **ellipse** (a slightly squashed circle), which means that the planet does not always maintain the same distance from its parent star. At **perihelion,** the point in our orbit when we're closest to the Sun, we receive about 7 percent more sunshine than we do at **aphelion,** the point at which we're farthest away. (For those of us in the northern hemisphere, perihelion actually occurs in winter, which means that our winters don't get as cold as they could if things were the other way around.)

Of the solar energy that reaches Earth's atmosphere, about 30 percent bounces right back into space, reflected by the tops of clouds. Another 20 percent is sponged up by particles floating around in the upper atmosphere, and about 3 percent is reflected away by shiny bits on the Earth's surface, like oceans and snow fields. All in all, we actually receive only about half of the solar radiation that comes our way — which, for the most part, is plenty.

Hot Crickets, Cold Crickets

Some animals act as natural thermometers. The best known of these is probably the cricket, whose friendly chirping speeds up or slows down depending on how hot or cold it is. (Actually, the chirping sound is made by male crickets scraping their wings together; they're hoping to attract mates.) You can figure out the temperature from cricket chirps using a special formula:

$$T = 50 + (N - 40) \div 4$$

In this equation T is the temperature in degrees Fahrenheit (F) and N is the number of cricket chirps in one minute. This formula is called **Dolbear's Law** after A. E. Dolbear, the entomologist who discovered it in 1897.

Crickets aren't the only animal thermometers. The rate at which ants crawl is also directly related to temperature. So is the rate at which rattlesnakes rattle.

Engine in the Sky

T he Sun is the engine behind the world's weather machine. Energy from the Sun stirs the world's winds, warms the currents of the world's oceans, and gives us day, night, and changes of season. Solar energy can also be harnessed to generate electricity.

Solar, or photovoltaic, cells use semiconductors such as silicon to convert light energy from the Sun into electricity. These are the cells used to operate solar-powered calculators. They're also used in the solar panels on house rooftops and on satellites, and they've even been used to power cars.

Solar energy is clean, inexpensive, and inexhaustible. The Sun, after all, pours it on us every day for free, at the rate of 100 watts per square foot per second. One

World Record

In summer 2000, a Canadian solar-powered car called the Radiance covered 4,375 miles in 29 days, using about as much power as it takes to run a toaster.

problem with using solar energy as a source of electricity, though, is that not every area gets enough sunshine. For example, sun-soaked Arizona might do just fine, but light-deprived Alaska and rain-drenched Seattle would be in trouble. Also, solar cells aren't yet all that efficient. But scientists are working on them. Solar energy is a bright hope for the future.

The Global Greenhouse

The **greenhouse effect** is good. Without it, all life on Earth would have frozen solid long ago or, more likely, never have started in the first place. "Greenhouse effect" refers to the way our atmosphere behaves like the glass ceiling and walls in a greenhouse, capturing heat and reflecting or radiating it back to the planet's surface. A problem arises only when there are too many greenhouse gases, which can create a runaway greenhouse effect and lead to climate-disruptive global warming.

Green leaves are like little solar collectors. They sop up energy from sunlight and use it to convert carbon dioxide and water into sugar and oxygen. This is a complex biochemical process called photosynthesis.

All our food ultimately comes from photosynthesis. Whether you're a meat-eater or vegetarian, what you're really eating is sunlight packaged by plants.

Photosynthesis

Photosynthesis takes place in the **chloroplasts** of plant cells. The chloroplasts contain a special green pigment called **chlorophyll** that absorbs solar energy and converts it into the chemical energy needed for making sugar.

The chemical formula for photosynthesis looks like this:

$$6CO_2 + 6H_2O + \text{solar energy} \rightarrow C_6H_{12}O_6 + 6O_2$$

Here is a picture of my garden.

Seeing Spots

There are times when we don't seem to get quite enough sunshine. This might have something to do with **sunspots,** the dark splotches that sometimes appear on the Sun's bright surface. Astronomer Theophrastus of Athens wrote about sunspots in 300 B.C., and the Chinese were recording them as early as 28 B.C., but Galileo usually gets credit for their discovery. He was the first to describe sunspots in detail, making maps of their shifting shapes and keeping track of their movements across the face of the Sun. Early observers suggested that the spots were everything from holes in the Sun to solar mountaintops. One particularly impressive set of spots, noticed in A.D. 807, was thought to be an omen predicting the death of Charlemagne. (If so, it was predicted very far in advance; Charlemagne died in A.D. 814.)

We now know that the mysterious spots are really huge magnetic storms — some bigger than the entire planet Earth — that appear and disappear and reappear again in (on average) an 11-year cycle. During the solar maximum, hundreds of sunspots are seen and the Sun is wildly active, spouting flares and belching massive plumes of gas. During the solar minimum, few spots are visible and the Sun's surface is relatively quiet.

Many observers have claimed that the sunspot cycle affects the world's weather, but just how it does — or even if it does — isn't clear. Low sunspot activity, though, does seem related to lower solar radiance: that is, when there aren't any sunspots, the Sun gets dimmer; and when the Sun gets dimmer, the Earth gets cold.

Between 1645 and 1715, for example, the Sun produced hardly any sunspots at all. This period, known as the **Maunder Minimum** after the scientist who first studied it, is also called the Little Ice Age. Temperatures fell so low that glaciers began to creep southward; there were widespread crop failures and famines; and the water in the canals of sunny Venice froze solid. Studies indicated that a **Maunder Minimum** occurs every 200 to 300 years, and some astrophysicists predict that we're due for another sometime in the 21st century.

MAKE YOUR OWN SUN PEEPER

What you'll need:
- **A pushpin**
- **Two white paper plates**

Galileo damaged his eyes studying sunspots because he used his telescope to peer directly at the Sun. He was lucky he didn't go blind. Solar astronomers use special protective filters to study the Sun. For a safe look at the Sun, try building your own Pinhole Sun Viewer.

1. With the pin, poke a hole in the middle of one of the paper plates.

2. Go outside and hold the pinhole up to the Sun. Don't look at the Sun. Hold the plate so that the Sun is behind you, shining through the pinhole.

3. Hold the second plate in front of you and move it until you see an image of the Sun projected on the paper. You might have to move it up and down until it comes into focus.

PINHOLE SUN VIEWER

What you'll need:

- Scissors (or an X-Acto knife)
- An empty cereal box
- A sheet of waxed paper
- Transparent tape
- Duct tape
- A pushpin

1. Cut a flap in the front of the cereal box, cutting across the middle of the box, down one side, and then across the bottom. The flap should lift up like a lid.

2. Cut a strip of waxed paper the same width as the bottom of the cereal box but about 4 inches longer. With transparent tape, attach the ends of the strip to the inside of the box, parallel to the bottom and about 2 inches up.

3. With the pushpin, make a hole in the center of the bottom of the cereal box.

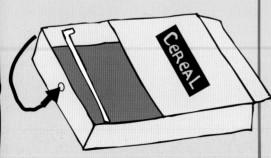

4. Close the flap (1) and tape it shut with duct tape. Cover all sides of the flap with tape. You want this box to be dark inside.

5. Cut the flaps off the top of the box. This is the end of the box that you will look through when pointing the pinhole toward the Sun.

6. Look into the open end of the box and squeeze it tightly around your face to block out as much light as possible. You want to keep things dark.

What happens: You should see an image of the Sun on the waxed paper screen inside the box.

SPLITTING SUNLIGHT

What you'll need:

- A sunny day
- A shallow dish (try a pie plate)
- A small mirror

1. Fill the dish about half full of water.

2. Dunk the mirror in the water and angle it into the sunlight.

What happens: You should be able to see a rainbow reflected on a nearby wall. If you can't wait for a sunny day, try shining a bright flashlight on the angled mirror and catching the rainbow on a sheet of white paper or an index card.

"Sometimes we see a cloud that's dragonish;
A vapor sometime like a bear or lion,
A towered citadel, a pendant rock,
A forked mountain, or blue promontory
With trees upon it."

– William Shakespeare

Chapter Four

Clouds

White Sheep
& Little Cat Feet

The atmosphere, as a global whole, generally contains about 2 percent water. Just exactly how much water individual packets of air hold, however, depends on the temperature. Cold air holds hardly any water at all; warm air sops up water like a sponge. The icy air of Antarctica holds less than 0.1 percent water vapor; the steamy air over a tropical rain forest contains up to 3 percent. Air at 80°F on a warm summer day can hold five times as much water as air at 32°F on a chilly morning in winter.

"Evaporation gets blamed for a lot of things people forget to put the top back on."

– a student

Jumping Water Molecules

Air contains water because water continually jumps into it. At the invisible molecular level, water, even in the quietest puddle, is always in movement with molecules bouncing and bumping against each other like crazed herds of miniature bumper cars. At the water's surface, some of these jumpy molecules periodically bounce too far, tear themselves loose from the group, and hurtle off into the atmosphere. This process is called **evaporation** and the amount of evaporated water in the air at any given time is referred to as **humidity.**

A Cloud Is Born
Warm breath on a cold day will condense into a cloud.

If you've ever seen steam billowing out of the spout of a teakettle or have watched your breath form white puffs in the air on a cold winter day, you've seen a cloud in the making. Evaporated water can also fall back out of air again, **condensing** into water droplets, and condensation is the secret behind clouds. When you blow a breath into the frosty air in winter, warm air from your lungs, filled with water vapor, hits the cold outer air and instantly cools. The now-cold air is no longer able to hang on to its water vapor, which promptly condenses into water droplets, producing a little white cloud.

The same thing happens when clouds form in the upper atmosphere. Warm vapor-filled air from the Earth's surface rises, spurting up through the atmosphere like a fountain, and as it rises higher and higher into the sky, it cools. Eventually it cools so much that it can no longer hold its cargo of evaporated water. At this point the water condenses. Molecules clump together to form tiny water droplets, and these condensed water droplets — trillions of them — make clouds.

If the humidity hits 100 (percent), the air has absorbed as much water as it possibly can. This doesn't put you underwater. Rodney does not understand this. If he did, he would not be running around in his swimming trunks.

RELATIVE HUMIDITY

Meteorologists usually report humidity as **relative humidity**, which is a percentage. They divide the actual amount of water in the air by the total amount of water that that air could possibly hold at that temperature. Relative humidity changes if the amount of moisture changes or if the temperature of the air changes.

Today the air is hot and sticky. Jemima says this is because the humidity is high. Humid air contains a lot of water.

How Do You Dew?

Dew on the grass in the evening and early morning is also the result of condensation. As warm water-laden air contacts the cool ground, it cools to the point where it can no longer hold its burden of water. For the same reason — condensation — drops of water form on the outside of a cold glass of lemonade sitting on a picnic table in the hot sunshine.

Often meteorologists determine the amount of water in the air by measuring the **dew point.** The dew point is the temperature at which a given sample of air is completely saturated with water — that is, the temperature at which the air holds as much water as it possibly can. In other words, the dew point is the temperature at which relative humidity is 100 percent. For example, take a nice warm water-vapor-filled sample of 85°F air. If you start cooling down that air, it will gradually become less and less able to hang on to its water vapor because cold air can hold less water than warm air can. Eventually you'll reach a temperature, say 50°F, at which the air becomes just too cold to hang on to its water vapor. At this point the vapor condenses and forms a cloud. You've reached the dew point.

Rodney is all wrong about cotton candy. Cotton candy is made of sugar. Clouds are made of tiny water droplets. Sometimes Rodney can be very silly.

Many poets have written about fog. T. S. Eliot described "the yellow fog that rubs its back upon the windowpanes"; Carl Sandburg said fog moves on "little cat feet."

Fog is the lowest cloud of all, a cloud that seems to crawl along the ground — or the water, as in the case of the famous fog of San Francisco that rolls in daily from the Pacific Ocean. The first to write about San Francisco's fog was Sir Francis Drake, who became stuck in it for a full month in 1579 while sailing around the world in his ship, the *Golden Hind.* The fog was so thick and persistent that it prevented Sir Francis from discovering San Francisco Bay.

Fog of this sort occurs along most of the world's coastlines. It forms when moisture-filled air moves horizontally over a cold surface, such as the cold water of the Atlantic or Pacific or the chilly water of lakes and rivers. Such thick creepy stuff is known as **advection fog;** it often reduces visibility to zero, brings traffic to a halt, and causes endless delays at airports.

Radiation fog, or **ground fog,** is also white, thick, and low and can have similar traffic-thwarting effects, but it forms under different circumstances. After sunset, the Earth cools rapidly, radiating the heat built up during the day back into the atmosphere. If the cooling air near the ground contains enough moisture, water vapor will condense to form a layer of ground fog. It usually disappears by midmorning as the Sun heats the land and "burns it off."

London fog — the eerie ooze through which Sherlock Holmes pursued criminals and Jack the Ripper stalked victims — is more properly dubbed **smog,** a mix of natural fog and coal smoke. Before laws were passed restricting the burning of coal, smog formed a yellowish city-wide cloud that could last for days, so heavy and thick that it was often referred to as "pea soup." Today smog remains a problem, especially in heavily populated and industrialized areas, though now it usually results from automobile exhausts and power plant emissions.

A? Q? I?

AQI stands for Air Quality Index, which is a measure of pollutants in the air. The AQI scale runs from 0 to 500, and the higher the number, the gunkier the air. AQI values of 50 and under indicate that air quality is good; values over 150 are unhealthy for everybody.

A Drink of Fog

California's towering red-wood trees get most of their water from coastal fog, and scientists now suggest that areas of the world that have little drinking water might also be able to use the same source to collect theirs. Along the coast of Chile, huge mesh nets serve as fog-catchers, collecting tiny water droplets out of the air.

Killer Clouds

Although the worst most clouds do is get you wet, some kinds can be downright lethal. Volcanic clouds are boiling blasts of steam, ash, and gas belching from erupting volcanoes that kill everything in their path. The leftover debris, tossed high into the upper atmosphere, can block incoming sunlight and cool Earth's climate for years and even decades.

So much ash and dust were thrown into the stratosphere by the monstrous eruption of Indonesia's Mount Tambora in 1815 that the season following was known long after as "the year without a summer." There were crop failures and famines worldwide; and in New England, snow fell in July.

The 65-million-year-old asteroid impact that killed half of all species of life on Earth — including the dinosaurs — did most of its damage by means of a dust cloud. The aftermath of the collision, scientists calculate, threw a cubic mile of dust into the atmosphere, where it remained for months, blocking 99 percent of the available sunlight.

Cloud Talk

When we speak of a cloud on the horizon, we mean there's trouble ahead. We also say that every cloud has a silver lining, which means there's something hopeful to be found in even the gloomiest situation.

Sometimes that something hopeful is rain.

Clouds in Space

Earth isn't the only planet to have clouds. Mars has a scattering of thin clouds made of ice crystals and dust, and Venus is completely wrapped in a 12-mile-thick blanket of yellowish poisonous clouds made mostly of hydrochloric and sulfuric acids. Giant Jupiter and Saturn have colorful bands of clouds composed mostly of ammonia. Aquamarine-colored Uranus and turquoise blue Neptune have glittery white clouds made of methane.

MAKE YOUR OWN HYGROMETER

What you'll need:

- **Scissors**
- **A piece of heavy cardboard about 12 inches long and 9 inches wide (from the side of a cardboard box)**
- **A piece of thin cardboard, poster board, or a large index card**
- **A pushpin**
- **A 1-foot-long strand of hair**
- **Glue**
- **A dime**
- **A straight pin**
- **A hairdryer**

The amount of water in the air is measured using a **hygrometer**. In 1783, Swiss physicist Horace Benedict de Saussure invented a mechanical hygrometer using plain ordinary human hair. Hair expands or contracts with the humidity, changing length by as much as 3%.

1. Cut two ¼-inch-long slits 1 inch in from the left on the top (9-inch) side of the piece of heavy cardboard.

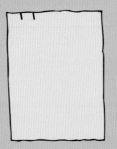

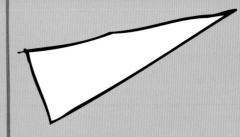

2. From the thin cardboard, cut a triangular pointer about 6 inches long.

4. Attach the pointer to the heavy cardboard with the pushpin. The pointer should be located 3 inches up from the bottom of the heavy cardboard, with the wide part against the left edge. Position the pushpin about ½ inch from the edge, in the center of the pointer.

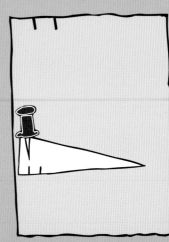

3. Cut two small slits at the bottom of the pointer about 1 inch from the left (wide) edge.

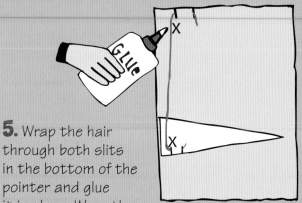

5. Wrap the hair through both slits in the bottom of the pointer and glue it in place. Wrap the other end of the hair through the slits in the upper edge of the heavy cardboard. Glue the hair in place.

6. Glue a dime 1½ inches from the left edge of the pointer base.

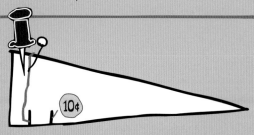

7. Put the straight pin through the hole in the pointer (next to the pushpin) such that the hair is just stretched when the pointer is horizontal.

8. Find the 100% humidity mark on your hygrometer by taking it into the steamy bathroom while you shower. Mark the position on the hygrometer.

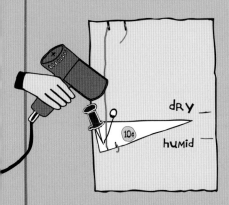

9. Then dry the hair thoroughly with a hair dryer and mark the position for 0% humidity on your hygrometer.

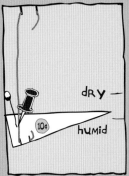

10. Now you're ready to monitor daily humidity.

Cloud in a bottle

What you'll need:

- Water
- A spray bottle
- An empty 2-liter soda bottle
- A match

Get a grown-up to help you with this one!

1. Spray some water from the spray bottle into the soda bottle so that there is a coating of water droplets on the inside.

2. Light the match, blow it out, and drop it into the bottle.

3. Seal the bottle tightly and press down firmly on the outside of the bottle for a minute or so. Then let go.

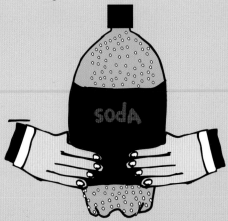

4. When the cloud forms, open the bottle and squeeze.

Make A Psychrometer

What you'll need:

- **Scotch tape**
- **Two bulb thermometers, marked in degrees Centigrade**
- **Gauze or a cotton ball**
- **Small rubber band**
- **Small fan**

1. Tape the two thermometers side by side to the edge of a table with the bulb ends extending over the edge of the table about 1 inch (2.5 cm).

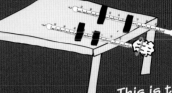

This is the "dry-bulb" thermometer.

This is the "wet-bulb" thermometer.

2. Wet the gauze or cotton ball and fasten it with the rubber band around the bulb of one thermometer.

4. Note the temperatures on both thermometers.

dRy bulb 21°C

weT bulb 19°C

2°C

5. Subtract the wet-bulb reading from the dry-bulb reading.

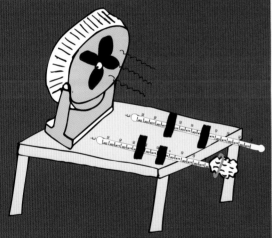

3. Blow the fan on the thermometers until the liquid in the tubes stops falling.

6. On the following chart, find your dry-bulb temperature reading on the left and the difference (see **5**) on the top. The point where these intersect on the chart is the relative humidity in percent.

Relative Humidity Table (in percent)

Dry Bulb   **Dry Bulb Minus Wet Bulb (degrees celsius)**

°C	1	2	3	4	5	6	7	8	9	10
10	88	77	66	55	44	34	24	15	6	
11	89	78	67	56	46	36	27	18	9	
12	89	78	68	58	48	39	29	21	12	
13	89	79	69	59	50	41	32	22	15	7
14	90	79	70	60	51	42	34	25	18	10
15	90	81	71	61	53	44	36	27	20	13
16	90	81	71	63	54	46	38	30	23	15
17	90	81	72	64	55	47	40	32	25	18
18	91	82	73	65	57	49	41	34	27	20
19	91	82	74	65	58	50	43	36	29	22
20	91	83	74	67	59	53	46	39	32	26
21	91	83	75	67	60	53	46	39	32	26

Chapter Five

"The mist and cloud will turn to rain,
The rain to mist and cloud again ..."

- Henry Wadsworth Longfellow
"Keramos"

Rain

Drops, Drizzles & Downpours

"Into each life some rain must fall," wrote poet Henry Wadsworth Longfellow in 1842 — and a good thing it does, because without it all the land on Earth would be desert. Since ancient times, cultures worldwide have invented rituals, ceremonies, entertainments, and outright tricks intended to convince the gods to send rain.

Too much rain, on the other hand, can be as bad as or even worse than too little. The ancient Hawaiians appealed to their rain god, Lono, at one temple to bring rain in times of drought; at another they prayed to get rid of rain in times of flood.

The First Rain

Where did rain come from in the first place? Water, most geologists guess, originally came out of the Earth starting about four billion years ago. As the young molten planet cooled and solidified, water vapor leached out of the hot rocks in a process known as **outgassing.** The steamy vapor rose until it hit the cool air of the upper atmosphere; then it condensed and fell, for thousands of years, as rain, drenching the newly forming continents and filling the empty bowls of the oceans. That very same water, most scientists believe, is still around today, filling our lakes, rivers, wells, and reservoirs and falling on us as rain.

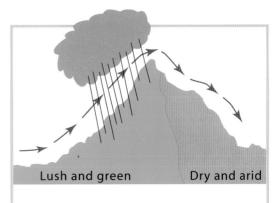

Lush and green   Dry and arid

Rain Shadow
Clouds dump their rain on the windward sides of mountain ranges, leaving the leeward sides (usually the eastern sides in North America) high and dry.

Ice Balls from Space

One theory proposes that Earth's water arrives in giant ice balls from outer space. Based on evidence from satellite photographs, Louis Frank, a physics professor from the University of Iowa, suggests that the Earth is being steadily bombarded with huge cosmic ice balls. About 25,000 chunks of ice, each the size of a small house, may zing toward our planet every day.

Some regions of the globe receive a lot more rain than they need; others, hardly any. If you're hoping for rain, the place to be is on a windward coastal slope near warm tropical waters or on the windward side of a mountain.

In such drippy locations, the mountains boost vapor-laden air upward, causing it to expand and cool. This forces the water vapor to condense and fall as rain. For example, rising air dumps all its rain on the western slopes of the Rockies, leaving the unlucky eastern side of the mountains to struggle by on less than ten inches of rain a year. The side of mountains away from the prevailing wind is said to be in a **rain shadow.**

Forty Days and Forty Nights

The most famous rain in the Bible is the one that fell for 40 days and 40 nights, drowning the world in water and floating Noah's animal-laden ark. A flood of this sort, one brought on by lots and lots of rain, is referred to by meteorologists as a **traditional flood.**

Recent archaeological evidence, however, suggests that Noah's flood may not have been traditional at all. Geologists Walter Pitman and William Ryan guess that the story may come from a monster flood that occurred 7,000 years ago, when water from melting glaciers caused the Mediterranean to break spectacularly through the barrier separating it from what is now the Black Sea.

Today it is raining. Rain is part of the water cycle or hydrological cycle. This is how it works:

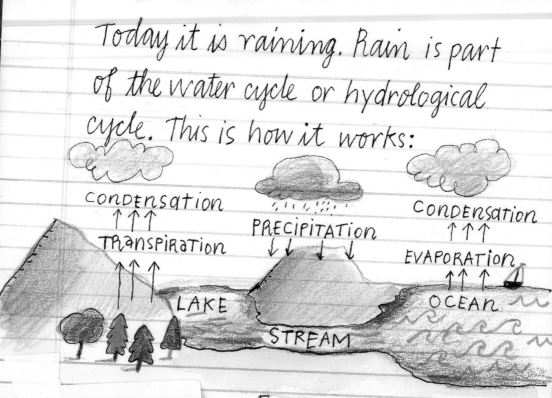

CONDENSATION
↑ ↑ ↑
TRANSPIRATION
↑ ↑ ↑

PRECIPITATION
↓ ↓ ↓ ↓

CONDENSATION
↑ ↑ ↑
EVAPORATION
↑ ↑ ↑

LAKE

STREAM

OCEAN

Water Facts

The water cycle has been going on ever since Earth's oceans formed, about 3.8 billion years ago. Water molecules falling in raindrops over your backyard have a long history. They were drunk by thirsty dinosaurs, filled the marble baths of ancient Rome, fell on the Crusaders, and watered the Pilgrims' first fields of corn.

About 75% of the Earth is covered by water and of that water 97% — is in the oceans. Altogether, there are about 326 million cubic miles of water on our planet. At any given time, about 3100 of those cubic miles are found in the atmosphere.

First water evaporates from oceans, lakes, rivers, and puddles, and transpires from plants. High in the atmosphere the evaporated water condenses and forms clouds. When the teeny water droplets in the clouds get big and heavy enough, they fall as raindrops.

Jemima

The raindrops eventually collect in puddles, rivers and lakes, and oceans and then evaporate again. Water is never wasted. It just keeps going around and around. Rodney does not appreciate the hydrological cycle.

He is writing poetry.

I ONCE READ A POEM ABOUT RAIN
IN WHICH THE WORDS FELL DOWN
JUST LIKE FALLING RAINDROPS
JEMIMA SAYS THIS IS SILLY
SHE DOES NOT LIKE POETRY

Rodney

Raindrops & Hailstones

Rain, whether you've got a lot of it or just a little, begins as minuscule droplets of water in clouds. As the droplets bump around in the upper atmosphere, they begin to stick together and coalesce. As more and more droplets merge, they grow steadily larger and heavier. By the time they're hefty enough to fall as raindrops, they're up to 15 million times their original size.

Illustrations often show raindrops as teardrop-shaped — that is, round on the bottom and pointy on the top. Real raindrops, however, don't have points. Small drops are perfect spheres, like miniature marbles. Larger drops are heavy enough that they might squash a bit due to gravitational forces, which give them the shape of tiny hamburger buns.

Meteorologists classify rain according to the size and number of the falling raindrops. A **drizzle,** for example, averages about 14 raindrops per square foot per second, each about .04 of an inch in diameter, accumulating on the ground at the halfhearted rate of .01 inch per hour. A **cloudburst,** on the other hand, throws down 113 drops per square foot per second, each drop .1 inch across, accumulating at the rate of 4 inches per hour. If you're out in a cloudburst, chances are you're wet.

In the steamy tropics, raindrops start and end their lives as splashy liquid water. Over the temperate zones, however, the droplets that ultimately become rain begin in the frigid upper atmosphere as ice crystals. As the falling crystals hit the warm air closer to the Earth's surface,

Dancing in the . . . Milk?

Gene Kelly's dance with his umbrella in the 1952 motion picture *Singin' in the Rain* actually took place on a movie set. Tarps overhead made it look like nighttime; sprinklers provided the rain, which was mixed with milk so it would show up better. The result was the most famous and joyful dance number in movie history.

they melt; by the time they reach our roofs, heads, hats, or umbrellas, they've become rain. Under certain conditions, though, temperate raindrops stay solid.

During storms, when conditions in the upper atmosphere are wild and turbulent, falling raindrops can be caught in updrafts and flung back skyward, where they freeze into icy pellets. Depending on the rowdy behavior of air currents within the clouds, these pellets can be passed up and down like bouncing balls, repeatedly thawing and freezing, building up layer after layer of ice like the successive layers of an onion. Eventually the frozen little pellets become heavy enough to fall, clattering to the ground as **hail.**

Most hailstones measure just half an inch or so across, the size of a small gumdrop or a large blueberry. Periodically, however, storms produce monster hailstones, big enough and hard enough to be potentially lethal. The worst hailstorm on record showered hailstones the size of billiard balls on villages near New Delhi in India in 1888, killing 246 people and more than 1,600 cattle, sheep, and goats.

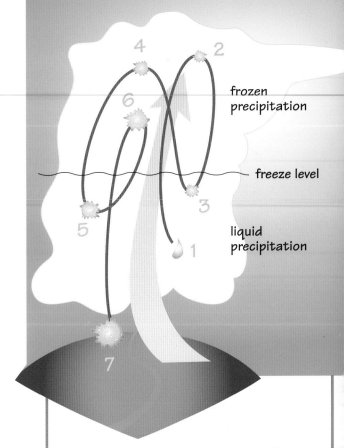

frozen precipitation

freeze level

liquid precipitation

A Hailstone's Travels

Inside a storm cloud a raindrop (1) can be blown upward, freeze (2), and fall again (3). Bouncing up and down (4, 5, 6), it adds layers of ice until it becomes heavy enough to fall as hail (7).

Golf ball–sized hailstones are not unusual. The largest hailstone on record in the United States, however, was about the size of a grapefruit and fell on Coffeyville, Kansas, on September 3, 1970. It weighed 1.67 pounds and measured 17.5 inches around.

It's Raining FROGS!

In 1882, a hailstone containing a pair of frogs fell on Dubuque, Iowa (after the ice thawed, the frogs sat up and hopped away); and in 1894, a ball of ice containing a six-inch turtle fell on Vicksburg, Mississippi. The frogs and turtle aren't alone. Animals raining (or hailing) unexpectedly from the sky have been a feature of weather lore since ancient times.

Pliny, writing in the first century A.D., mentions rains of milk, blood, wool, and even baked bricks. A rain of herring fell on Scotland in 1821; snails fell on Chester, Pennsylvania, in 1870; mussels rained on Paderborn, Germany, in 1892; frogs fell on Trowbridge, England, in 1939; and in a Yuma, Arizona, rainstorm in 1941, a boy was bopped on the shoulder by a falling clam.

Best guess for the cause of such weird rains is probably **waterspouts** (tornadoes over water) that fling unfortunate fish (etc.) into the upper atmosphere. This may also explain the rain of frozen ducks that fell in 1973 over Stuttgart, Arkansas. Meteorologists guess that the unlucky ducks were scooped up by a tornado and thrown to such high altitudes that they iced over.

FACT! Red rains of "blood" most likely result when raindrops form around flecks of reddish iron-containing dust picked up by desert windstorms. Yellow or "sulfur" rains come from raindrops wrapped around yellow grains of airborne pollen.

Acid Rain

Raindrops can combine with air pollutants to create acid rain. About 10 percent of the pollutants responsible for acid rain come from natural sources, such as volcanic eruptions and forest fires. The rest comes from car exhausts, industrial smokestacks, furnaces, and power plants.

Even normal rain is a little bit acidic. **Distilled water** (absolutely pure water) is neutral: that is, it has a pH level of 7.0. Ordinary rainwater has a pH of about 5.6 — mildly acidic — because carbon dioxide gas in the air dissolves in the water in raindrops to make carbonic acid, a very weak acid.

Acid rain, however, contains dissolved pollutants, such as sulfur dioxide and nitrogen oxide, which combine with water to form strong acids: corrosive sulfuric and nitric acids. Acid rain can have a pH as low as 4.3, which is about as acidic as a tangy tomato. Such rain has many damaging effects on forests, lakes, and rivers and their resident plants and animals; it can also slowly dissolve stone buildings, especially those made from acid-sensitive marble or limestone.

The Acid Test

Chemists use the pH scale, which runs from 0 to 14, to determine how acidic or basic a solution is. A pH of 7, right in the middle of the scale, is neutral. Anything with a pH below 7 is acidic, and the lower the pH, the more acidic it is. Tomato juice has a pH of 4; lemon juice, 2; and battery acid, 1. A pH above 7 means a solution is basic, like seawater (8), ammonia (12), and drain cleaner or lye (13).

In the United States, rain is most acidic in the Northeast, due to windblown pollutants from factories in the Midwest.

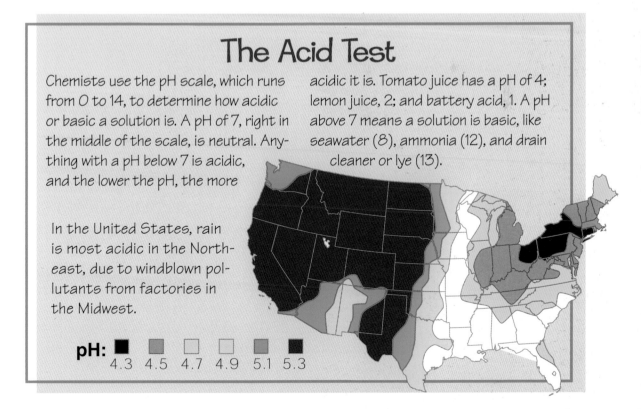

pH: 4.3 4.5 4.7 4.9 5.1 5.3

What Shape Is a Rainbow?

After the rain, if you're lucky, you might see a rainbow. The best time to spot one is right after a rainstorm. Stand facing the departing storm, with your back to the sun. In North America, rainbows are seen most frequently in the afternoon, when the prevailing winds are shoving the clouds and rain eastward and the sun is shining through in the west. The later in the afternoon, the better. When the sun is low on the horizon, the bow of the rainbow will be larger.

An Irish folktale claims that the leprechauns bury their gold at the end of the rainbow. Actually (leprechauns are tricky) there is no real end to the rainbow. In the first place, the rainbow is a trick of light. It forms when sunlight is **refracted** (bent) and reflected by falling raindrops. Raindrops act like tiny prisms, splitting white sunlight into its component colors — red, orange, yellow, green, blue, indigo, and violet (ROYGBIV) — and then reflecting the colors back toward the ground (and to your eyes).

In the second place, a rainbow is round. The bow-shaped arch of color we see from the surface of the Earth is just a piece of the circle. The center of the rainbow circle — the **antisolar point** — is below the horizon, at a distance equal to the height of the sun above the opposite horizon. This means that the higher the sun is in the sky, the farther the antisolar point is below the horizon. When the sun is high, the rainbow will look smaller because we're seeing a smaller section of the circle.

The higher you are, the more of the rainbow you'll be able to see. From an airplane, you can see the entire endless circular bow.

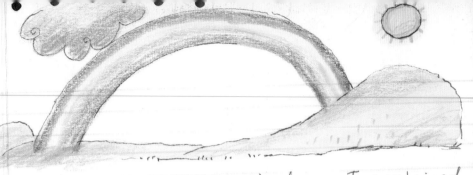

Today we saw a rainbow. I explained to Rodney how rainbows work. But Rodney was too excited to listen. He kept running around yelling about buried treasure and looking for a shovel. Rodney is gullible.

HOW RAINBOWS WORK

Rainbows happen because raindrops act like tiny prisms in the air. When sunlight passes through a raindrop, the water causes the light to bend or **refract**. White sunlight is made up of many different colors — red, orange, yellow, green, blue, indigo, and violet — and each color is a different wavelength of light. Each wavelength bends a different amount when passing through water droplets. Violet light bends the most and red light bends the least.

We see a rainbow as big bands of color in the sky because we only see one color from each raindrop. Each raindrop refracts light into all its different colors but the drops are positioned so that only one of those colors is at the right angle to reach an observer's eye.

How can you ever find a pot of gold if you don't look for it?

Ice Storm!

An ice storm isn't really a storm of ice; it's a particularly nasty form of rain. Ice storms can occur anytime from late October to early May, when a wave of warm moist air sweeps north from the tropics, eventually bumping into a layer of freezing-cold high-pressure air in the upper latitudes. As the two air masses make contact, the warm southern air begins to cool. Its water vapor condenses and begins to fall as what would ordinarily hit the ground as snow.

Under special ice storm conditions, however, the snow — on its way down — passes through that layer of warm air still moving up from the south and melts into rain again. Then, as it nears the chilly ground, the falling drops become super-cooled — that is, the temperature of the water in the raindrops falls below the freezing point (32°F or 0°C) while still remaining liquid. When these super-cooled drops hit the cold Earth, colliding with roofs, trees, sidewalks, and roads, the shock of the impact triggers freezing.

The result is a glittering glaze of ice covering everything in sight, turning parking lots into skating rinks and highways into bobsled runs. Tree branches tinkle like wind chimes in their encasing coats of ice — or, if enough ice accumulates, branches, telephone lines, and power cables will sag and break under the strain. Dazzlingly beautiful ice storms are among the most dangerous and destructive forms of weather.

MAKE YOUR OWN RAIN

What you'll need:

- A saucepan
- Water
- A stove
- A pie plate
- Ice cubes
- Oven mitts

GET A GROWN-UP TO HELP YOU WITH THIS ONE!

1. Fill the pan with water, put it on the stove burner, and bring the water to a boil.

2. Fill the pie plate with ice cubes.

3. Hold the pie plate over the steam that rises from the boiling pan.

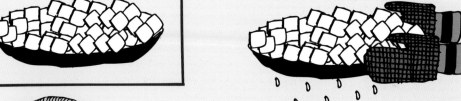

Use oven mitts — steam is very hot and can scald you.

4. Watch what happens.

What happens: The rising steam - water vapor - condenses when it hits the cold surface of the ice-filled pie plate, just as evaporating water vapor from the Earth's surface condenses when it reaches the cold temperatures of the upper atmosphere. When the condensed water droplets grow large and heavy enough, they will fall (or rain).

MAKE YOUR OWN RAINSTICK

What you'll need:

- Colored markers
- Cardboard tube from a paper towel roll or (better) a wrapping paper roll
- 1-inch nails
- Masking tape
- Two index cards
- Uncooked rice or small beans

1. With a dark-colored marker, draw small dots, about half an inch apart, in a spiral around the length of the tube.

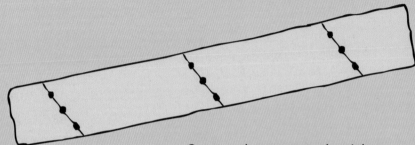

Some tubes are made with a spiral seam, which can be used as a guideline.

2. Push a nail through each dot into the center of the tube (but don't go all the way through to the other side).

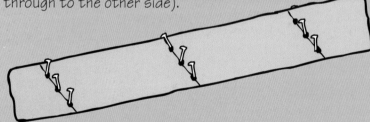

3. Wrap tape around the tube to hold the nails in place.

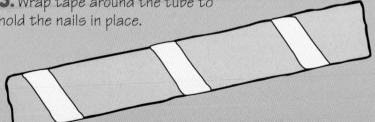

The Diaguita people of Chile, who live in one of the very driest places on Earth, made rainsticks from dried cactus stems filled with pebbles. The rattle of the pebbles sliding back and forth inside the sticks sounded like a rainstorm and was supposed to alert the neglectful rain gods.

4. Cut a circle from an index card, just slightly larger than the open end of the tube. Place it over one end of the tube and tape securely in place. The end of the tube should be sealed shut.

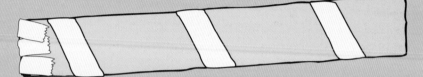

5. Standing the tube on end, pour half a cup of rice or beans into the open end of the tube.

6. Repeat step 4. Cut a second index-card circle and tape over the open end of the tube. Tape securely to seal shut.

7. Decorate the outside of the tube with colored markers. (*Optional*: Glue colored feathers to one end of the tube.)

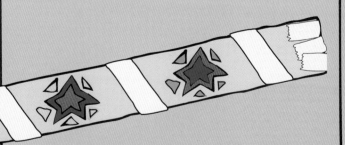

8. Tilt the tube back and forth and listen to the sound of falling rain.

MAKE A RAIN GAUGE

What you'll need:

- A printed rain gauge OR a 6-inch plastic ruler
- Heavy-duty clear tape
- A straight-sided glass jar

1. Cut out rain gauge and laminate or seal in heavy-duty clear tape.

2. Set rain gauge or plastic ruler inside the jar, so it rests on the bottom and stands upright. Secure the top with tape.

3. Place jar outside in an open area, supported so that it will not fall over.

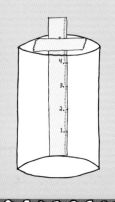

4. After each rain, record your measurement, then empty the glass.

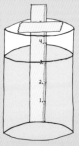

MEASURING A RAINDROP

What you'll need:

- A nylon stocking
- A large juice or coffee can
- A heavy rubber band
- Powdered sugar

1. Cut a piece of stocking large enough to cover the top of the can. Pull it tightly over the top of the can and secure it with the rubber band.

RAINING PICKLE JUICE?

What you'll need:

- **2-ounce plastic cup**
- **pH test strips (available from science or educational supply companies)**

1. Each time it rains, collect a sample of rainwater in your cup.

2. Dip a pH test strip in your water sample.

3. Record the results.

RAiN dATe	
3 / 5	5.3
3 / 7	4.9
3 / 9	5.1

2. Sprinkle a layer of powdered sugar smoothly over the nylon.

3. Put the can out in the rain for a few seconds. The raindrops will dissolve the powdered sugar, leaving spots that correspond to the size of the drops.

"Thunder is good, thunder is impressive;
but it is lightning that does the work."

— Mark Twain

Chapter Six

Thunder & Lightning

Thor's Hammer & Zeus's Spear

If you've got a sunny personality, you have a cheerful and pleasant disposition. If you think things are right as rain, you're happily satisfied with life in general. If you've got a face like a thundercloud, on the other hand, you're probably furious.

A thunderstorm is about as close as nature gets to a full-fledged temper tantrum, with spectacular special effects: roars, bellows, booms, fireworks, and explosions.

It's Electric!

To the Vikings, storms were the fault of Thor, the touchy red-headed god of thunder, rumbling across the sky in his goat-drawn chariot and flinging his magic hammer, Mjolnir, which pulverized everything it hit. To the ancient Greeks, lightning bolts were spears hurled by an angry Zeus. Many North American Indian tribes claimed storms were the work of the Thunderbird, whose flapping wings made the thunder and whose eyes shot bolts of lightning.

Actually, thunderstorms come from cumulonimbus clouds. In the hot muggy days of summer, the Earth soaks up heat from the Sun and radiates it back into the atmosphere, creating huge, warm, light-

Thunderbird

weight air masses that rise buoyantly into the air. As they rise, they create a pressure imbalance beneath them, near the Earth's surface. More air rushes in to fill the low-pressure gap, warms up in turn, and heads for the upper atmosphere. The air — the raw material of the building thunderstorm — is like an immense hot fountain bubbling slowly into the sky.

As the hot air reaches the higher altitudes of the troposphere, it cools and condenses to form a cloud. This massive conveyor belt of upward-moving hot air ultimately thuds up against the tropopause, the temperature barrier at the very top of the troposphere, 40,000 feet or more above the ground.

There the swelling cloud stops dead and starts to spread out, turning itself into a towering monster with a flat, anvil-shaped top. The thunderstorm is ready to roll.

Thor, Viking god of thunder

We are having a thunderstorm.

I am writing this from underneath the bed.

The cat is here too.

We are keeping safe. Jemima is not keeping safe. She is sitting at her desk.

She says she will be all right because

1. She is not standing under a tree.
2. She is not near a window.
3. She is not in contact with a telephone, plumbing, or electrical wires,
4. She is wearing sneakers.

Jemima says going underneath the bed is silly.

I will miss Jemima.

Bolts from the Blue

A thundercloud is a seven-mile-high tower of turbulent wind, rain, and hail. It's also an electrical explosion waiting to happen. Inside the cloud, for reasons meteorologists don't yet quite understand, electrical charges separate, sorting themselves out so that the looming top of the cloud is primarily positively charged while the threatening bottom of the cloud is primarily negative.

At the same time, positive charges begin to build up on the ground beneath the cloud. Ordinarily air is an excellent **insulator:** that is, electricity can't move

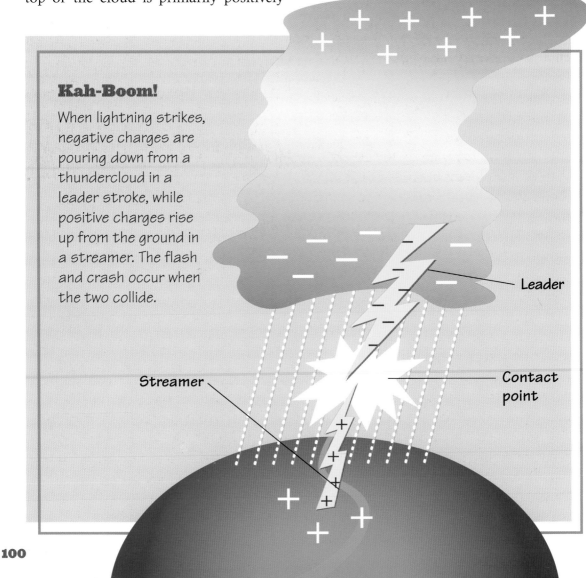

Kah-Boom!

When lightning strikes, negative charges are pouring down from a thundercloud in a leader stroke, while positive charges rise up from the ground in a streamer. The flash and crash occur when the two collide.

Leader

Contact point

Streamer

through it. An electrically charged thundercloud, however, is too powerful for the insulating properties of air to handle. Eventually huge negative charges build up to the point where something simply has to give.

Lightning, to the nervous observer, may look like a single blazing zap from overhead, but actually it proceeds in a series of stairlike steps. Lightning begins as a 200-(or so)-foot-long **leader** of negative charges, extending downward from the bottom of the thundercloud. The negative charges in the leader are strong enough to ionize the air, converting it from a stodgy insulator to a charged plasma, capable of conducting electricity. The leader carves a conductive path toward the earth's surface, one 200-foot step at a time, at a rate of 100 miles per second. This process takes only a few thousandths of a second, but for lightning it's the equivalent of a laid-back saunter. Things soon get much faster.

About 100 feet above the Earth's surface, the downward-heading train of negative charges meets its mate — a **streamer** of positive charges nosing upward from the ground below. The meeting is spectacular. The result is an instantaneous and massive electrical discharge. Negative charges by the trillions hit the ground — the lightning **strike** — and positive charges from the streamer–leader **contact point** rocket back into the sky at a blinding rate of 75,000 miles per second. It's this upward-speeding **return stroke** that we see as a bolt of lightning.

Never Say Never

The old saying that lightning never strikes twice in the same place isn't true. In fact, lightning strikes repeatedly in the same places, especially if those places happen to be the tallest things around.

The Empire State Building in New York City, for example, is struck by lightning about 23 times each year. During one thunderstorm, the building was struck eight times in just 24 minutes.

I have explained to Rodney that statistically we are safe from lightning as long as we do not do something stupid like running outside holding golf clubs over our heads.

But Rodney will not come out from under the bed.

He does not trust statistics.

The channel that lightning follows through the sky is narrow (less than an inch across) and, with the passage of the return stroke, it becomes very hot. It's this heat that we see as the lightning flash — a scorching sliver of air heated to a phenomenal 50,000°F, five times hotter than the surface of the Sun. Air, heated, expands; and the air of the lightning channel, instantaneously heated to enormous temperatures, expands so rapidly that it literally explodes. The shock wave produced by this explosion is what we hear as **thunder.**

Most lightning doesn't actually hit the ground. About 80 percent of the lightning in a thunderstorm is **cloud-to-cloud lightning,** flashing between charged areas within or between clouds. This can wreak havoc with electronic guidance systems in unluckily placed airplanes, but it isn't a problem for people down below.

However, the remaining 20 percent — **cloud-to-ground lightning** — definitely is. There are more than 2,000 thunderstorms occurring at any given moment worldwide, firing off eight to ten million cloud-to-ground lightning strikes daily. Your chance of lethally connecting with one of these depends on where you are.

Your chance is best (or, rather, worst) in Africa. The lightning capital of the world is tropical Africa, which averages more than 280 thunderstorm days each year. In the United States, the lightning hot spot is central Florida, with up to 100 annual thunderstorm days. The Great Plains, in contrast, average thirty to fifty thunderstorms each year; the New England states have ten to thirty; and the coast of California, five.

When lightning does hit, the results can be devastating. More than two thirds of all forest fires are set ablaze by lightning strikes, and a well-placed bolt of lightning can wipe out power and telecommunications networks. Worse, lightning kills people (between 100 and 300 Americans every year) and injures up to 1,500 more.

Great Balls of Fire

Sometimes lightning takes the form of fizzy glowing spheres about the size of grapefruit. Such rare and bizarre **ball lightning** appears in association with thunderstorms, hovering, floating, rolling, bouncing down stairs, or even occasionally exploding.

Flash and Boom!

One place not to stand during a thunderstorm is outdoors in the middle of it. You're safest by far from lightning when you're inside a building or a car.

If you're in water, get out of it. Water conducts electricity. So do metal objects. If caught in a thunderstorm, put down your golf club, tennis racket, sword, or umbrella and stay away from metal fences.

If you're absolutely stuck outside, don't be near — and don't *be* — the tallest thing around. Keep away from isolated trees: They may look like a protective shelter, but trees can attract lightning.

Your best bet is to keep as low as possible while minimizing your contact with the ground. Put your feet together and crouch down, lowering your head.

FACT! The catastrophic explosion of the Hindenburg over Lakehurst, New Jersey, in 1937 was caused by lightning igniting the flammable paint of the zeppelin's outer cover.

Ben Franklin's Kite

The man who first demonstrated the electrical nature of lightning was Benjamin Franklin, in his famous experiment in 1752 involving a kite, a June thunderstorm, and a metal household key. Launched into the storm, the key picked up enough of a charge of electricity to send a shock through Franklin's arm.

The kite wasn't actually hit by lightning; if it had been, Franklin wouldn't have been around afterward to tell the tale. The electrical current in the average lightning bolt peaks at 30,000 amperes. Just to compare: Ordinary household electric current is 110 amperes. It only takes 0.1 ampere to kill you.

Oak struck by lightning

The oak's peculiar problems with lightning are due to its rough, ridged bark, which prevents the oak tree from becoming uniformly wet. Ordinarily when lightning hits a tree, it first contacts the tree's uppermost branches and then, if the tree is wet, will follow the surface water film to the ground. The oak's bumpy bark, however, tends to keep parts of the oak's outer surface dry.

When the descending lightning bolt hits a dry spot, it leaps to the next-best downward-conducting path, the watery sap channels inside the tree. The heat of the passing lightning vaporizes the sap, which expands violently, causing the unlucky oak to explode. Many trees do manage to recover from lightning strikes, but often all that's left of the oak is a shredded stump.

Any tree can be dangerous during a thunderstorm, but the most dangerous of all is the oak. Oaks are struck by lightning more than any other tree. To the ancient Greeks, oaks were sacred to Zeus, famed for his flinging of lightning bolts; to the Vikings, the oak was sacred to Thor, god of thunder.

Lightning Rods

The first really effective anti-lightning device, the lightning rod, was invented by Benjamin Franklin, who described it in an article titled "How to Secure Houses from LIGHTNING" published in *Poor Richard's Almanack* in 1753. Franklin's lightning rods are still used — and still work — today.

The metal rods (which are sometimes called **points** or **air terminals**) are spaced along the highest point of a building and connected to each other by a long metal cable. The cable also connects to a **ground terminal,** usually a ten-foot metal rod driven deeply into the ground. In the event of a lightning strike, the rods provide a safe path for the incoming bolt, shooting it down the cables and plunging it harmlessly into the earth.

Tornado!

Particularly powerful and long-lived thunderstorms are known as **supercells.** These weather giants, bigger and meaner than the average storm, can produce not only lightning and thunder, but terrifying tornadoes as well.

The United States is the world leader when it comes to tornadoes. About 800 tornadoes touch down here each year, most in the Midwest. The stretch of territory extending from Texas to Nebraska, prime stomping ground for supercells, is known as Tornado Alley. It was a tornado roaring down Tornado Alley in Kansas that picked up Dorothy and Toto, house and all, and transported them to Oz.

Watch or Warning?

A tornado watch means that the weather conditions are right for tornado formation. A tornado warning means that a tornado has been spotted and is on the move.

As in any thunderstorm, a rising column of air forms the core of a supercell. Here, though, the fountaining air, prodded and buffeted by turbulent winds, begins to rotate as it climbs, forming what meteorologists call a **mesocyclone.** As the mesocyclone spins faster and faster, air pressure at its center drops from the sea-level average of 14.7 pounds per square inch to as low as 12.5.

Warm moist air promptly roars in to fill this low-pressure gap and is yanked upward at speeds of more than 100 miles per hour. The mesocyclone grows larger and larger, turning itself into a towering funnel-shaped tube of dizzily spiraling air.

Under low pressure, air in the center of the tube also expands and cools and the vapor in it condenses. The resulting cloud is what initially makes the tornado visible. At this stage it looks like a lethal spinning trumpet, poking downward, mouth-

Tornado Alley

In an average year, 800 tornadoes hit the United States, causing 80 deaths and 1500 injuries.

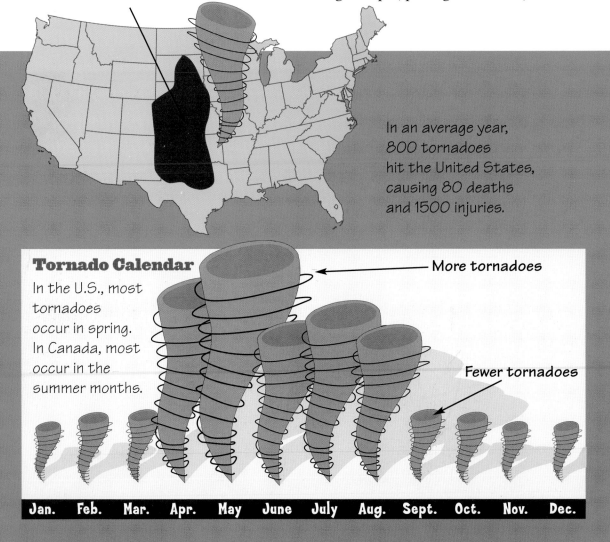

Tornado Calendar

In the U.S., most tornadoes occur in spring. In Canada, most occur in the summer months.

More tornadoes

Fewer tornadoes

| Jan. | Feb. | Mar. | Apr. | May | June | July | Aug. | Sept. | Oct. | Nov. | Dec. |

piece first, from the bottom of a cumulonimbus cloud. It's officially designated a tornado when it hits the ground.

Tornadoes don't amount to much in terms of size. Most measure just a few hundred feet across, which is a drop in the bucket as far as storms go. Thunderstorms are generally 5 to 15 miles wide. Hurricanes (more than a thousand times bigger than tornadoes) can be anywhere from 200 to 500 miles across. What a tornado lacks in size, however, it makes up in awful behavior.

Tornadoes are impressively destructive. They contain the most violent winds on Earth, up to 300 miles per hour or more, strong enough to blow anything in their path to bits. They're also, often, flat-out strange.

Tornadoes have been known to pluck the feathers off chickens, drive straws through tree trunks, yank blankets off beds without disturbing the sleepers, and pick buildings off their foundations, turn them around, and set them back down again. One tornado sucked a refrigerator

Funnel developing

Mature tornado

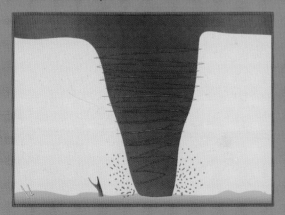

Touch down

Dissipating or decaying

out of a kitchen, carried it half a mile, and dropped it on the roof of a bank. Another hoisted a crate of eggs, moved it 500 yards, and set it down again without cracking a single shell. Tornadoes also snap trees like matchsticks, explode houses, smash cars and trucks, and topple trailers.

Based on the amount of destruction left in a tornado's wake, meteorologists Theodore Fujita and Allen Pearson devised the Fujita-Pearson Tornado Intensity Scale, which allows observers to determine just how dreadful a tornado really was. Even the puniest tornadoes — F0 on the Fujita-Pearson Scale — are pretty horrendous. These are designated **gale tornadoes** and feature winds of 40–72 mph, able to tear down chimneys and break branches off trees.

Higher-level tornadoes get steadily worse. F1 tornadoes are **moderate;** F2, **significant;** F3, **severe;** and F4, **devastating.** The most powerful tornadoes, F5 on the Fujita-Pearson Scale, are referred to as **incredible.** These winds of 260 to more than 300 mph can tear apart houses and fling trucks through the air.

Even the strongest tornado eventually blows itself out. Some last just a few minutes; others persist for a few hours. And most don't move very far, covering on average 5 to 15 miles of ground.

When a tornado is at its peak, it's a solid-looking cloud, with its fearsome funnel nearly perpendicular to the ground. As it peters out, however, it begins to sag and shrink, drooping sideways until — finally — it seems to lift and disappear back into the sky.

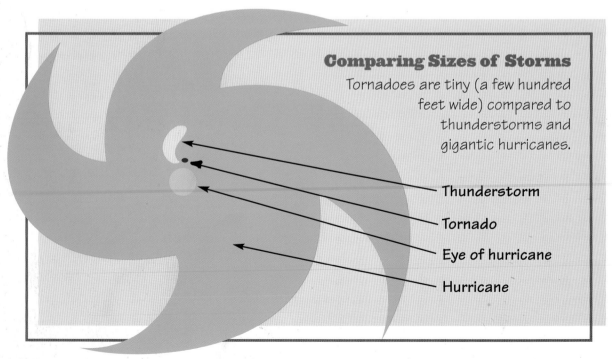

Comparing Sizes of Storms

Tornadoes are tiny (a few hundred feet wide) compared to thunderstorms and gigantic hurricanes.

Thunderstorm

Tornado

Eye of hurricane

Hurricane

TORNADO iN a BOTTLE

What you'll need:

- Two 2-liter plastic soda bottles
- A "Tornado Tube" connector, available from most scientific supply companies OR a 3/8-inch metal washer and electrical tape

1. Fill one of the bottles about two-thirds full with water.

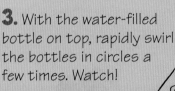

2. Connect the two bottles by screwing the "Tornado Tube" in place OR place the metal washer between the mouths of the two bottles and fasten firmly in place by wrapping with electrical tape.

TAPE

WASHER

3. With the water-filled bottle on top, rapidly swirl the bottles in circles a few times. Watch!

4. For a more spectacular effect, add food coloring or glitter to the water.

What happens: A funnel-shaped tornado-like vortex will form as the water drains from the upper bottle to the lower.

LiGHTNING ON A PLATE

What you'll need:

- **Thumbtack**
- **Aluminum pie plate**
- **Pencil**
- **Glue**
- **Chunk of Styrofoam**
- **Wool sock or mitten**

1. Push the thumbtack up through the center of the pie plate.

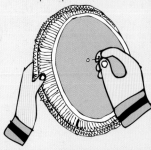

2. Push the end of the pencil onto the tack.

Use glue if you have to. You'll be using this as a handle.

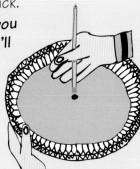

3. Rub the Styrofoam rapidly with the wool mitten or sock.

4. Lift the pie plate with the pencil handle and set it down on top of the Styrofoam. Do *not* touch the pie plate with your hands.

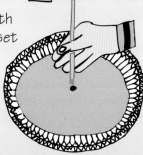

5. Turn out the lights and carefully bring your finger close to the pie plate. ZING! You should see (and feel) a tiny leaping lightning-like spark.

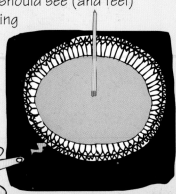

What happens: As you rub the Styrofoam with the mitten, it picks up electrons from the wool and becomes negatively charged. Since like charges repel, when you place the aluminum plate on top of the Styrofoam, all the electrons on the plate get as far from that negatively charged Styrofoam as they can – out toward the edge of the pie plate. When you bring your finger close to the edge of the plate, those electrons leap across the gap to your finger, giving you a teeny shock.

HOMEMADE THUNDER

What you'll need:

- **A foot-square (12 inches by 12 inches) piece of corrugated cardboard (try cutting one from the side of a cardboard box)**
- **A knife**
- **A triangle of brown paper (14 inches by 14 inches by 20 inches)**
- **Tape**

1. Score the cardboard square from corner to corner diagonally with a sharp knife. Be careful not to cut all the way through.

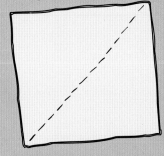

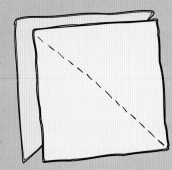

2. Place the cardboard square on top of the brown-paper triangle as shown. Fold the paper over the sides of the cardboard and tape securely.

3. Fold the cardboard in half along the scored line with the paper triangle folded inside it.

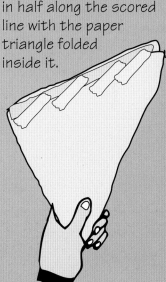

4. You're ready to thunder! Hold the cardboard by the end opposite the paper triangle, raise it over your head, and swing down fast.

BANG

For a more spectacular effect, decorate your thunder machine with felt-tip markers, paint, stickers, or glitter.

Chapter Seven

"Announced by all the trumpets of the sky,
Arrives the snow . . ."

– Ralph Waldo Emerson "The Snowstorm"

Snow & Ice

Frost, Flurries & Blizzards

People can never quite make up their minds about snow. Some think it's wonderful stuff. Lovers of snow compare it admiringly to soft blankets, glittering stars, or delicate feathers.

Others, especially those who have to shovel it, think snow is a cold nuisance. Some even find it downright frightening. In old Norse tales, the Frost Giants from the wintry land of Jotunheim are eternal enemies of humankind, waging war with driving snow and blocks of ice.

Hexagons from Heaven

Snow, at heart, is artistically frozen water. The snowflake starts life as a hexagonal crystal — an icy six-sided polygon. This shape depends on the chemical formula for water. Water is a three-piece molecule, made of two (small) atoms of hydrogen and one (large) atom of oxygen. Put together, a molecule of H_2O looks a lot like a teddy bear's head: a fat oxygen face with a pair of hydrogen ears stuck on at angles. When the temperature hits freezing, that particular head-and-ears shape fits together to form a framework of inter-locked hexagons.

Snow crystals form from supercooled water droplets in the shivery innards of clouds, at temperatures as low as −40° F. When a droplet hits one of the teeny particles of dust, ash, or other material that fill the atmosphere, it latches on and freezes solid. What's more, it attracts other water droplets to do the same, all snapping together like microscopic Lego blocks to build a six-sided crystal of ice.

The Snowflake Man

Wilson "Snowflake" Bentley, born in Jericho, Vermont, in 1865, was the first person to take photographs of snowflakes through a microscope. All of his snowflake pictures were beautiful, but some snowflakes were especially marvelous, shaped like double flowers or Maltese crosses or frozen fireworks. Bentley called these his "wonder crystals." There was even one snowflake he called his "Good Luck" crystal because it was shaped like a lucky horseshoe.

The United States Weather Service eventually collected Bentley's **photomicrographs** of snow and published them in a now classic book, *Snow Crystals* (1931). (It's still in print.) His snowflake pictures became so very popular that they were copied onto cloth, wallpaper, stained-glass windows, and greeting cards. Tiffany's, the famous jewelry store in New York City, turned Bentley snowflakes into diamond brooches; and the Vermont Sled Company painted Bentley snowflakes on sleds.

Bentley traveled all over the country giving lectures about snowflakes, but he never liked leaving home in winter. He always said that the best snow fell on Jericho, Vermont, and he hated to miss a good snowstorm.

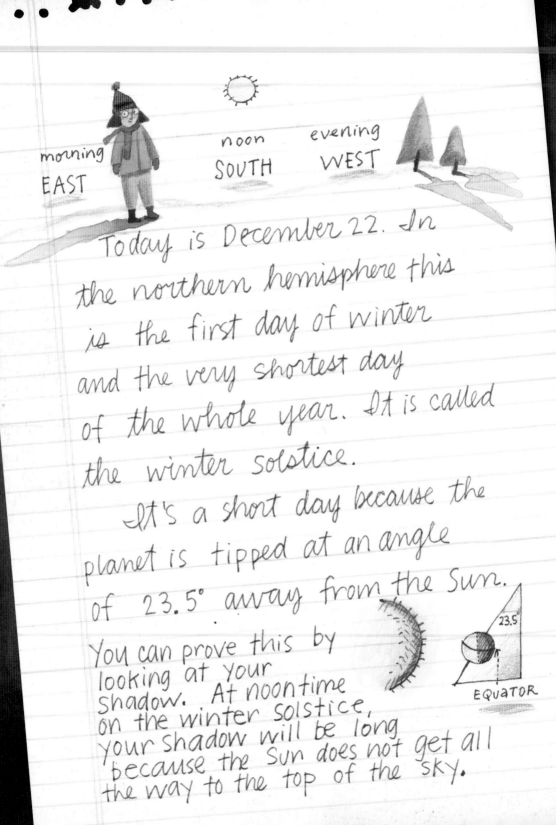

morning
EAST

noon
SOUTH

evening
WEST

Today is December 22. In the northern hemisphere this is the first day of winter and the very shortest day of the whole year. It is called the winter solstice.

It's a short day because the planet is tipped at an angle of 23.5° away from the Sun.

23.5°

EQUATOR

You can prove this by looking at your shadow. At noontime on the winter solstice, your shadow will be long because the Sun does not get all the way to the top of the sky.

morning
EAST

noon
SOUTH

evening
WEST

June 21, the summer solstice, is the longest day of the year. In the summer, the Earth is tilted toward the Sun and at noon on the summer solstice, the Sun will be at its highest point in the sky, almost directly overhead. Your shadow will be really short.

Sho

Great Snows

Snowflakes, one at a time, don't cause problems, but snowflakes by the trillions do. Weather history is filled with accounts of enormous life-disrupting snowfalls.

During a freak blizzard in Florence, Italy, in 1494, Michelangelo sculpted a fabulous snowman for his patron. In February 1717, the fabled Great Snow fell on Massachusetts, a ten-day marathon storm that dumped so much snow that houses were covered up to their chimney tops. Washington state holds the world record for annual snow, set in the winter of 1971–2 when a phenomenal 93.5 feet fell on Mt. Rainier. (That's enough to bury a six-story apartment building.) The average annual snowfall in Valdez, Alaska, adds up to 324 inches; Caribou, Maine, receives 111.9 inches; Flagstaff, Arizona, 100.3 inches; and Buffalo, New York, 92.5 inches. Denver gets 60.3 inches; and New York City, 22.9 inches.

On the opposite end of the scale, some places just plain don't get cold enough for snow. Atlanta averages only 2 annual inches of snow; Las Vegas just 1.2 annual inches; and Miami, Honolulu, and San Juan, Puerto Rico, receive no snow at all.

Snow is usually the result of a **cold front** — a heavy, leaden mass of cold air that oozes across the surface of the ground like a huge pool of cold molasses. When a cold front meets a mass of warmer, lighter air, it nudges itself underneath it, boosting the warmer air into the upper atmosphere. The moisture in this warm air mass, chilled, then condenses to form clouds and snow.

Snow doesn't always just fall. It sometimes also blows, piling itself into towering drifts and whipping horizontally through the air in such quantities that it creates whiteouts. According to the National Weather Service, if the temperature is rapidly falling, wind is blowing at a speed of 35 mph or more, and driving snow limits visibility to a quarter of a mile or less, you've got a **blizzard** on your hands.

The Worst Place in the World

The worst blizzards in the world are those of Antarctica, where wind speeds of 90 mph are common, with gusts up to 200 mph.

How Chilly Is Wind Chill?

Cold is bad enough all by itself, but it's worse with added wind. Cold air, moving, increases **convective heat** loss, which means that if you're outside in it, you get colder faster. **Wind chill** means that a blowing wind will make air temperature effectively colder than it really is.

To determine wind chill:

1) Multiply the wind speed by 1.5.

2) Then subtract the answer from the air temperature.

For example, if the wind is blowing at 20 mph and the temperature outside is 35°F:

$$20 \times 1.5 = 30$$
$$35 - 30 = 5$$

The wind chill factor is 5°F.

Pink as Driven Snow

If something is very white, we often say that it is as white as snow. Taken ice crystal by ice crystal, though, snow is not white but glassily transparent. The whiteness of a snowbank is a trick of light.

Not all snows, however, are snow-white. Snow can be practically all the colors of the rainbow: pink, red, blue, green, or yellow, and even brown or black. Brown and black snows form when water droplets crystallize around dark-colored dust particles. (A dismal black snow fell on the city of Chicago in the winter of 1947.) Yellow snow results when ice crystals form around yellow pollen grains.

Pink snow, found in the western Rockies and the Arctic, does not fall pink but is colored by microscopic plants called **cryophilic algae** — cold-loving relatives of pond scum. Other species of algae can tint snow blue, green, yellow, or red. Algae-red snow is said to smell like watermelon.

Seeing his Shadow

Winter officially ends around March 20, though snow, depending on your latitude and altitude, can hang on well into spring. Traditionally, the length of winter is predicted on February 2 by the neighborhood groundhog. He reputedly pokes his nose out of his den, sees his shadow, and retreats indoors, thus decreeing six more weeks of winter — or doesn't see his shadow, stays above ground, and declares winter at an end.

In real life, though, no sensible groundhog comes out of hibernation before the end of March.

HOW MUCH WATER?

What you'll need:
- A snowy day
- A straight-sided glass container

Did the 10:1 ratio work?

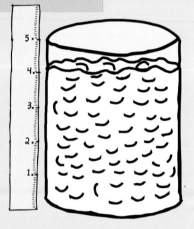

1. Collect newfallen snow in the container. Measure the amount of snow.

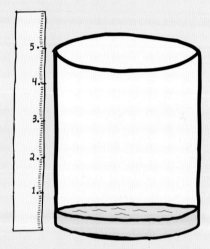

2. Let the snow melt. Measure the amount of water in the container.

Ten to One?

The traditional rule of thumb for determining the water content of snow is ten to one: that is, 10 inches of melted newfallen snow provides 1 inch of water. In practice, however, this doesn't work very well, since the water content of snow varies from place to place and from snowfall to snowfall.

The dry powdery snow that falls on the ski slopes of Colorado may only produce an inch of water for every 20 inches of snow, while the soggy, heavy snows of a New England spring may make an inch of water for every 3 inches of snow.

HOW TO STUDY SNOWFLAKES

What you'll need:

- A snowy day
- Black cloth (velvet works well) or a sheet of black construction paper
- Magnifying glass

1. Since snowflakes melt quickly, the trick here is to keep them cold. Put your piece of cloth or paper in the freezer to get it very cold before taking it outside.

2. Go outside, catch some falling flakes on the cloth or paper, and examine them with the magnifying glass.

3. A lot of your flakes will be broken — it's a hard trip down through the atmosphere — but you should eventually be able to see a number of different shapes and sizes. Maybe even a wonder crystal, just like Snowflake Bentley.

MEASURING SNOW

What you'll need:

- A ruler
- A straight-sided clear glass or plastic container (try a clear plastic soda bottle with the top cut off)
- Double-sided tape

1. Place the ruler inside the jar so that the measuring scale is visible from the outside. (Make sure the bottom of the ruler is on the bottom of the jar.) Tape the ruler securely in place.

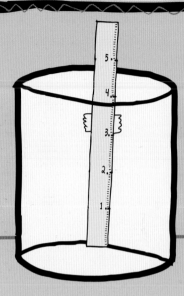

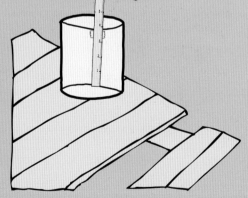

2. Place your jar outside in a flat, open area. (Secure it so that it won't fall over.)

3. After a snowfall, record the amount of snow in the jar. Then empty the jar and wait for it to snow again.

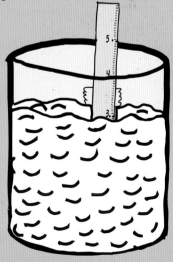

I have set up a weather station for collecting meteorological data. This is what it looks like:

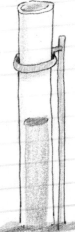

BAROMETER-
measures atmospheric pressure.

PRECIPITATION GAUGE-measures rain fall.

THERMOMETER-
measures air temperature.

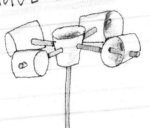

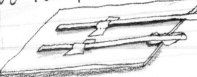

ANEMOMETER-
measures wind speed.

PSYCHROMETER-
measures relative humidity

WIND SOCK-
measures wind direction.

Predicting the Weather

Chapter Eight

Reading the Skies

Since ancient times, people have struggled to predict the weather. It can be a matter of life or death: Farmers must know about impending droughts, floods, or freezes; sailors about storms at sea; travelers about road conditions. Ancient weather predictions were based on dreams and visions, the appearance of the Moon, or the behavior of animals and plants. According to lore, you could tell a storm was coming because the bees buzzed more — or because seagulls hung around the beach, cows bellowed, pigs collected sticks, or spiders left their webs. If rain was on the way, cows lay down, owls hooted, and ants traveled in straight lines.

Some of these beliefs may have some basis in truth, but many of them don't. Cows bellow any old time. Seagulls usually hang around the beach, and bees buzz loudly whenever they are disturbed.

The first global theory of how weather really works was devised in the 1920s by Norwegian meteorologist Vilhelm Bjerknes and his son Jacob. Weather, Bjerknes believed, was a matter of moving air masses: that is, clouds, precipitation, and storms were all caused by the collision of moving blobs of cold and warm air. He compared this to war, and his weather descriptions are filled with talk of atmospheric invasions, attacks, victories, and defeats. Bjerknes called the boundary between moving air masses a **front,** the name given to the battle lines during World War I.

Woolly Bear Weather

According to time-honored legend, a wide middle stripe on a woolly bear caterpillar indicates a mild winter. Scientists, however, say the stripe story is pure myth. The width of the woolly bear's middle stripe varies with the age of the caterpillar and water levels in the area where it grew up.

Still, this doesn't stop believers. Vermilion, Ohio, holds a Woolly Bear Festival each summer, complete with a parade, woolly bear races, and official stripe measurements. The climax of the event is the announcement of the winter forecast.

This theory gave meteorologists the first useful tool for predicting (or at least giving an educated guess about) the weather. Once they knew the positions of current air masses and their directions of movement, observers could often figure out what would happen next.

When a mass of cold advancing air moves in on a mass of warm air (think of an enormous cold snowplow moving into a gigantic pile of warm ping-pong balls), the warm air retreats before the cold front and, being lighter, is boosted above it. At the meeting of the fronts, weatherpersons soon realized, there are likely to be storms: The warm rising air condenses as it reaches cooler altitudes to form clouds and rain.

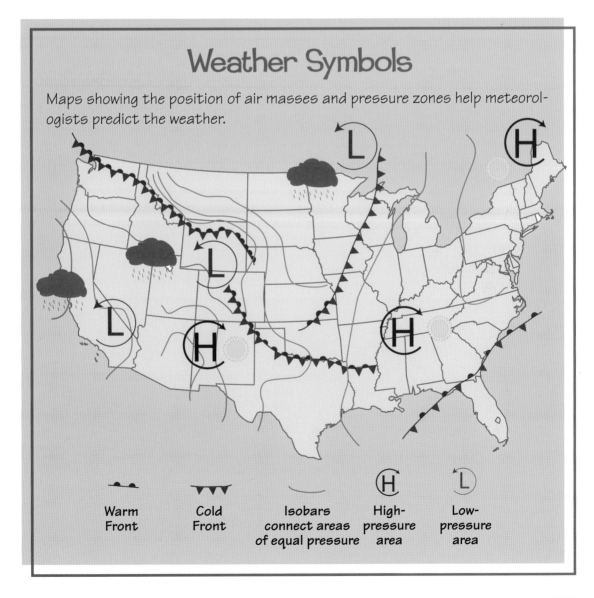

Weather Symbols

Maps showing the position of air masses and pressure zones help meteorologists predict the weather.

| Warm Front | Cold Front | Isobars connect areas of equal pressure | High-pressure area | Low-pressure area |

Satellite-generated data have given modern meteorologists a new global perspective. We no longer see weather as something that happens just in our own backyards. Events half a world away can determine how well our gardens will grow this summer and how much snow we can expect this winter.

Here's Looking at You

Geostationary satellites travel in **synchrony** with the Earth's rotation, which means they seem to stay in the same position above the Earth all the time. They orbit about 22,000 miles above the Earth's surface.

Sibling Rivalry

El Niño (a Spanish term for the Christ Child) is the name given to the warm ocean current that can appear just before Christmas off the coast of Peru, bringing with it heavy rains. Sea temperatures may rise so much that fish are driven away; torrential downpours cause mud slides and floods.

La Niña, the Child's little sister, begins when sea surface temperatures in the Pacific fall below normal. Where El Niño is known to scientists as a "warm event," La Niña is cold. This often ill-behaved pair seesaw back and forth every two to seven years or so. They can alter global patterns of atmospheric circulation from Darwin, Australia, to the island of Tahiti and beyond.

Rodney's Magic
Weather Rock

If the rock is dry, it is sunny.

If the rock is wet, it is raining.

If the rock is white, it is snowing.

If the rock is gone, it is windy.

Weather Terms

atmosphere Literally, "sphere of air" — the envelope of gases that surrounds a planet. The Earth's atmosphere is made up mostly of nitrogen and oxygen.

condensation When moisture in the air **(water vapor)** turns into water droplets. This happens as air cools. **Dew,** which forms as the air temperature drops, is an example of condensation.

convection In the atmosphere, the circular movement that occurs when air, warmed by the Sun, rises, leaving a gap beneath that cooler, denser air rushes in to fill. As the warm rising air cools at higher altitudes, it grows heavier and begins to fall. At the same time, the air beneath it warms up and begins to rise, repeating the pattern. This moving air creates **wind.**

convection cell A complete cycle of air warming and rising and cooling and falling.

Coriolis effect The process in which a moving object (such as an air current) is pushed off course by the Earth's rotation, to the right in the northern hemisphere and to the left in the southern hemisphere.

evaporation When molecules of liquid water pass into the air, turning into **water vapor.**

front The boundary between two different masses of moving air.

high-pressure zone An area where the weight of the air on the Earth is high. This is often associated with cool air and, since cool air is heavy, the weather in a high-pressure zone tends to be stable.

humidity The amount of moisture (evaporated water or water vapor) in the air.

low-pressure zone An area where the weight of the air on the Earth is low. This is usually because the air is warm. Since warm air is lighter, it naturally rises, and heavier, cooler air flows in underneath. Because of this pattern, the weather in a low-pressure zone is often changeable.

Weather Websites

- For a complete list of hurricane names, see the National Hurricane Center online at www.nhc.noaa.gov/aboutnames.html.
- For information on the Aeolian harp (wind harp), visit: www.exploratorium.edu/xref/exhibits/aeolian_harp.html and http://users.argonet.co.uk/artlute/aeol.html. To hear the sound of the harp, check out www.harpmaker.net/windharp.htm.
- For a variety of paper airplanes, helicopters, pinwheels, and other windblown creations, visit the following: www.exploratorium.edu/science_explorer/roto-copter.html www.paperairplanes.co.uk/heliplan.html www.smm.org/sln/tf/p/parachutingpinwheel/parachutingpinwheel.html www.thinkingfountain.org/w/whirlingwonders/whirlingwonders.html
- For more information on windmills and wind power, check the American Wind Energy Association at www.awea.org
- How hot is your hometown? See Weather Today at www.weathertoday.net/weather-facts.htm for a list of weather facts and figures.
- To find out today's sunspot number, view solar movies and animations, and learn when you might see a display of the northern lights, see Sunspots and the Solar Cycle at www.sunspotcycle.com.
- For a safe look at the Sun, try the Robotic Solar Telescope at www.eyes-on-the-skies.org or try building your own Pinhole Sun Viewer.
- For an interactive online pH meter, see the pH Factor: www.miamisci.org/ph/.
- To hear the sound of a thunder sheet and other weather simulation instruments, check out the Weather Simulation Machinery at www.phonyweather.com.
- For predictions of and information on severe weather in the United States, visit http://www.nssl.noaa.gov/.
- For tips on tornado safety, see http://www.tornadoproject.com/safety/safety.htm. For lightning safety, see www.lightningsafety.noaa.gov/.
- For more on Wilson "Snowflake" Bentley, the Snowflake Man, see www.snowflakebentley.com.
- For the National Weather Service Wind Chill Chart, check out www.nws.noaa.gov/om/windchill/.

Interior Photography Credits

Index

An *italicized* number indicates that a photo or illustration appears on that page.